AF581088

OLD DOGS, NEW CHAPTERS

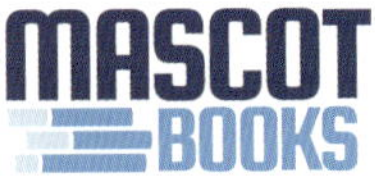

www.mascotbooks.com

Old Dogs, New Chapters: Uplifting Stories of Senior Rescue Dogs

Photo Credits:
Oatey and Gandalf: *Sarah Olsen, Once Upon a Van*
Harley and Phyllis: *Ruff Adventures in Austin, TX*
Leo: *Owen Woytowich Photography*

For more information, please contact:
Mascot Books
620 Herndon Parkway #320
Herndon, VA 20170
info@mascotbooks.com

CPSIA Code: PRTWP0919A
ISBN-13: 978-1-64543-097-1

Printed in Malaysia

Old Dogs, New Chapters is dedicated to the loving parents of senior rescue dogs past, present, and future.

OLD DOGS, NEW CHAPTERS

Uplifting Stories of Senior Rescue Dogs

ALISON CLARY & JASON PAPPAS

CONTENTS

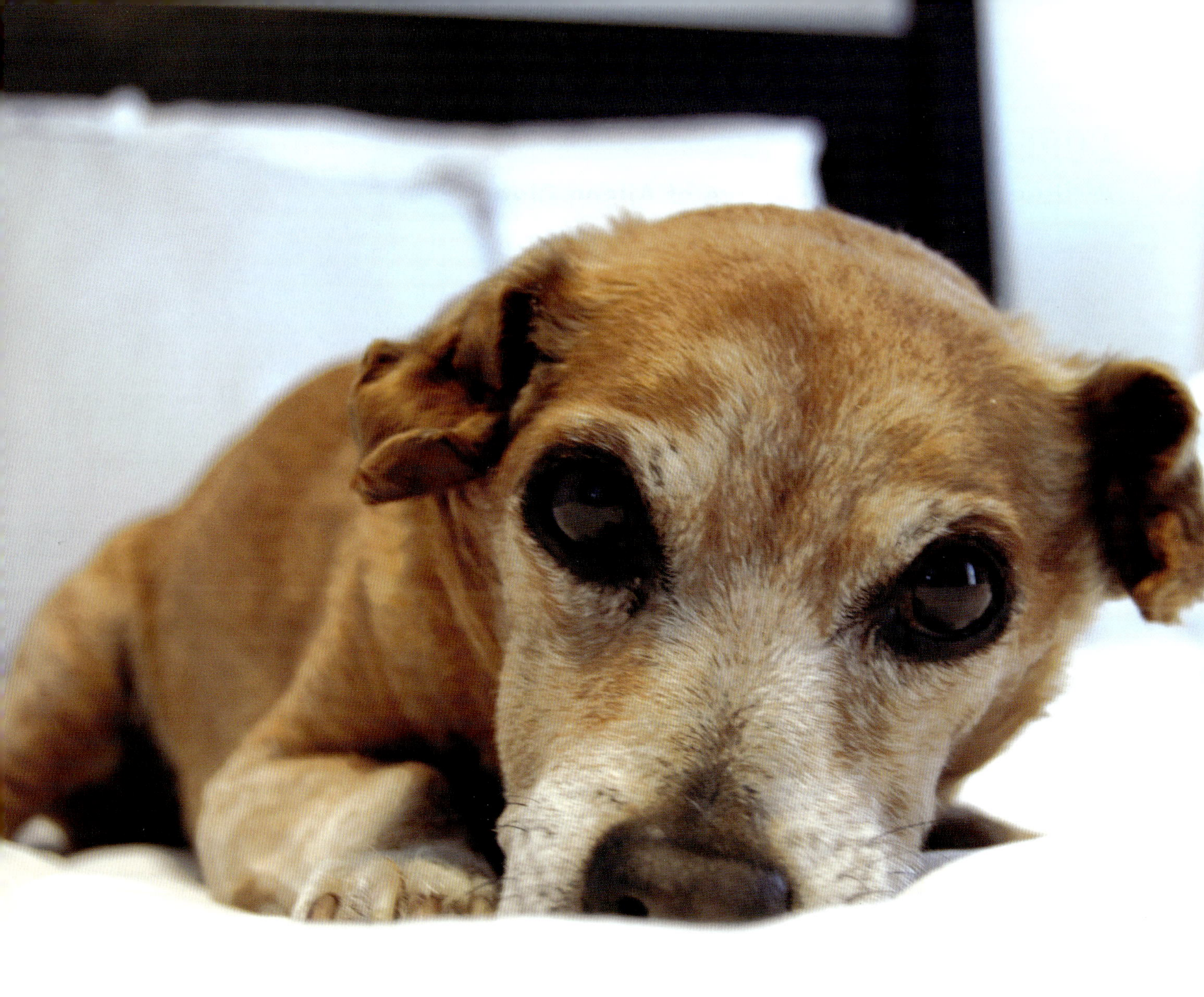

FOREWORD

Written from the perspective of Alison Clary

"We can tell by the signs on his body that Stanley has lived a hard life." This brief statement was the only narrative associated with Stanley's online adoption profile. Equally as disheartening as this concise description was the accompanying photo of a sad, little dog snuggled in a blanket amid a dull, gray background. His petite, tan body was missing patches of fur, and somehow, I could feel him shivering through the photo.

A few days passed after I initially stumbled upon Stanley's online adoption profile, but I could not shake the images of his massive black eyes or crumpled ears from my thoughts. Although there was no age listed with his profile, I could tell he was a senior—meaning he was at least eight years old—from the white markings that encroached his outer muzzle.

I was not completely certain it was the opportune time to adopt a dog, let alone a senior dog. Much of my future was unknown because I was in a long-term, long-distance relationship with my college sweetheart, Jason. Despite my undefined future, something deep inside was pulling me back to Stanley. I soon hopped into a car with my mom and embarked on the two-hour drive to visit Stanley at the Colonial Heights Animal Shelter.

When we arrived, my heart dropped as I saw an older gentleman standing outside Stanley's kennel. He was gently pressing his finger through the chicken wire gate and making sweet calls to lure Stanley towards him. Part of me was transfixed by the adorable scene I was witnessing. The other part of me was selfishly distraught that I had not arrived earlier.

Despite my attempts to hide my emotions, the man noticed my disappointment and kindly relayed that he had been looking for his lost dog for five years. He had seen Stanley's adoption profile and optimistically hoped he had finally found his beloved dog. As he approached Stanley's enclosure, he quickly realized Stanley was far too small to be his long-lost friend. "Please give him a good life," said the gentleman as he exited the shelter. I assured him I would.

As I sat with Stanley in the shelter, I realized he was in far worse shape than his online picture depicted. The shelter had taken good care of him, but their temporary nurturing was no match for the years of prior neglect his body had endured. He had a large tumor on his leg, he was missing more than half of his teeth, and his elongated nails resembled sloth's claws. He was also severely malnourished and had rope markings around his neck, which indicated he was likely tied up for a long period of time. Despite these many physical imperfections, I felt an immediate connection with Stanley and his gentle temperament. It was a raw and indescribable feeling, and I just knew we were meant to find each other. Luckily, Stanley seemed to agree; he delicately kissed my face as he wagged his brittle tail.

I was sold not only on Stanley, but on the life we could have together. While I was filling out an adoption application, I learned from the volunteer that Stanley was believed to be about ten and a half years old, and he had been found collarless, wandering the streets of Richmond, Virginia during a snowstorm. When no one came looking for him, they concluded he had been purposefully abandoned. Upon hearing this, I made a promise to him that he would never be abandoned again.

The first night with Stanley in my apartment went differently than I naively had expected. He whined persistently by the door, so I ended up taking him on nearly fifteen walks that night. By the time the twelfth walk came about, I was Googling "How long does it take a shelter dog to adjust to a new home?" The answer: six to eight weeks.

He ignored me every time I called his name that first night, and I wondered whether this was because he did not recognize the name the shelter had given him, or if he was purposefully avoiding me. Eventually, Stanley fell fast asleep in his cozy new dog bed, and I delicately tiptoed around my apartment so I would not wake him from his peaceful sleep. When it was time for me to head to sleep, I called Stanley's name so that he could join me in the human bed. He did not budge, so I began calling at a louder volume. I moved closer and closer, but he still did not move. I panicked when I noticed his tongue hanging out of his mouth.

I delicately tapped him on his head, and he leaped upward vigorously. I was so startled by his rapid movement that I fell backwards and bruised my thigh on the coffee table. After rising back to my feet, I quickly put the pieces together; Stanley was deaf. Consequently, I had not only adopted an aged, neglected dog, but I had also adopted a dog with special needs. I questioned whether I could handle this new discovery, but after looking into his giant eyes, I knew he was staying. We would figure it out together.

Over the next few weeks, Stanley began to ease into his new life and feel comfortable around me. His nightly walks went from an average of fifteen to around five. He started whining less, and his tail wagged a little more each time I returned home. I started learning that Stanley has many layers and moods. At times, he can be grumpy and stubborn, and other times he is playful and filled with puppy-like excitement.

As Stanley continued to settle into his new chapter, I began taking him to the vet regularly to treat his health issues. Each appointment, I learned of a new reason why Stanley looked and acted the way he did. I discovered his crumpled ears and deafness were the result of several painful ear infections that were left untreated. As for his limp...well, that was caused by several BB gun pellets lodged in his shoulder. After discovering these health issues were almost all rooted from prior neglect, I was astonished Stanley still was able to show me, and humans in general, so much love.

Together, our lives progressed a lot smoother. What I liked about our relationship was that we appreciated each other's company and did not judge each other's faults. As cheesy as it sounds, I felt my life had renewed purpose with Stanley around. Soon, in part due to this new feeling of self-assurance thanks to Stanley's presence, I found a job in Jason's town of Ocean City, Maryland and was hired soon thereafter. After receiving the offer letter, I had two weeks to pack up my belongings and settle into my new state. Stanley road shotgun on move day, sticking his head out the window the entire ride, and his calm demeanor really eased my nerves.

It has been a few years since Stanley and I moved across state lines. During this time period, I have noticed that his muzzle has whitened immensely, but his spirit has not wavered. He, Jason, and I now live in our first real home together. Jason has wholeheartedly accepted Stanley as his own, and trust me when I say that the feelings are reciprocated from Stanley's end.

Although Stanley has continued to age (as we all do), we have been surprised by how active and happy he still is. He enjoys frequent walks on the beach and running next to our bikes. We live adjacent to a local park, at which Stanley is considered a local celebrity. People with magnificently expensive purebred dogs walk through the park, but for some reason, quirky, old Stanley is the neighborhood kids' favorite dog. They stop mid-hide-and-seek to run over and present him with hugs and kisses.

We are asked frequently about why, as a relatively young couple, we have such an old dog. We kindly respond that we were meant to find Stanley, and his age did not play a role in us finding each other. We also make sure to say that while we helped Stanley find his new chapter, he helped us find ours also. This is usually followed up with the question, "Well aren't you going to be sad when he passes away?" The answer: of course. The unfortunate reality is that all dogs will eventually cross the rainbow bridge, and just because our time with senior rescue dogs is limited, it does not make our experiences together any less meaningful.

The truth is, adopting an older dog is both a rewarding and practical option. Senior dogs frequently are mild-tempered and have already been trained or know basic commands. They also do not require the constant careful watch that a puppy might. While the common perception is that the older the dog, the higher the vet bills, that is not always the case. Stanley, for instance, came to us already neutered, and many of his other vet-related costs were comparable to those expected with a new puppy.

There is also the emotional aspect to adopting a senior dog. Senior dogs who are up for adoption have likely seen things no dog should ever see. Sometimes they have been abandoned by their family, and other times, they never had a family to begin with. Often, they are confused by their situation and distressed. Despite this, senior rescue dogs are often just looking for one thing: love. They know what it is like not to feel love, so they are extra appreciative when it is shown to them.

Adopting a senior rescue dog also forces you to live in the present. You may not always know the details of their past or what their future holds, but you can always count on them to enjoy the present. If you adopt their mindset holistically, you can be sure you are living every day to the fullest.

In our opinion, all old dogs have a story to tell, especially senior rescue dogs. To pay tribute to our beloved Stanley and our experience in adopting him at an old age, we are recounting the true stories of other senior rescue dogs who are now enjoying blissful new chapters after being adopted later in life.

Through telling their tales, we hope to shine a light on the benefits of senior adoption and to shatter any false perceptions associated with rescuing an older dog. As you will see from these stories, you can certainly teach an old dog new tricks, and they can teach you some invaluable lessons about resilience and forgiveness as well.

THE DOGS

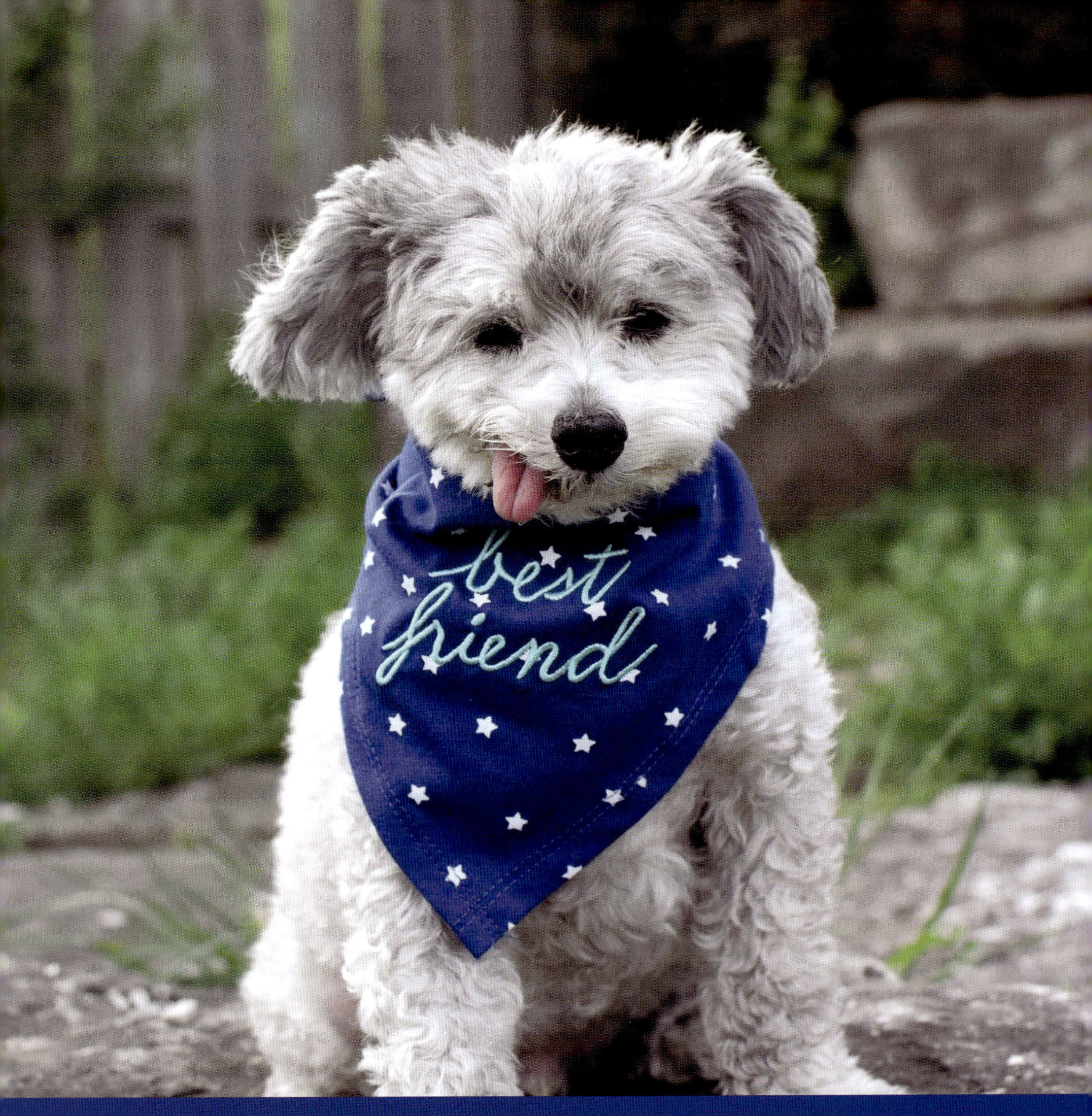
best
friend

WALLY, 11

Nowadays, Wally's daily adventures garner a large online fan base, but unfortunately, his life was not always so glamorous. The petite gray pup was found as a stray at nine years old, and it was suspected from his initial physical condition that he had been intentionally abandoned.

When Wally was swooped up by animal control, Kristen of Ontario was volunteering with a local rescue shelter and serving as a frequent foster mom. She received a photo of a disheveled older pup with a message asking if she would consider fostering him. Kristen knew almost nothing about him, not even his name. The only slivers of information provided were that he was a senior, and he appeared to be missing part of his bottom jaw. The lack of detailed information and Kristen's inexperience with senior dogs did not intimidate her, so she immediately agreed to foster him.

When Kristen arrived at the pickup location, she found a miniature plastic crate waiting for her. When she picked up the crate, she was stunned by its flimsiness, and she even physically looked to make sure there was actually a dog inside. After arriving home, she unfastened the crate and waited for a scruffy little grey ball of fluff to eventually venture out. After holding him in her arms for the first time, Kristen was aghast at how emaciated he was underneath the layers of matted fur. In fact, he was only about four pounds.

Wally's health was very unpredictable at the beginning, and at times, it was feared he might not make it. Despite the hefty uphill battle they faced, neither Kristen nor Wally gave up hope. The vet indicated he would need surgery to remove his remaining teeth and save what was left of his jaw. He was far too sick for surgery at that point, so he was given antibiotics and a food plan to help restore his weight.

He was a fighter, and with Kristen's diligent care, he grew stronger with each passing day. As his mobility improved, he started to become more active and playful. After a much-needed haircut and two months of steady improvement, Wally was finally healthy enough to undergo the risky, yet necessary, surgery. Fortunately, the operation was a success, and Wally could finally set his sights on reaching the finish line of his full recovery.

Wally's hair grew back curly, shiny, and soft, and he began embodying a teddy bear-like charm. Because he no longer had teeth, his tongue hung from his mouth adorably. He regained energy and about a month after his surgery, he was cleared by the vet as healthy enough for adoption.

In the three months that Kristen had been fostering Wally, she had been so focused on his recovery that she was not attuned to how deeply her love had grown for him. When the day came for his adoption profile to be posted online, Kristen felt anxious and sent a message to the adoption coordinator asking if they could talk. The next day, she signed his adoption papers and made their relationship official.

Over time, Wally's emotional well-being has caught up to his vast physical improvements. Witnessing his personality blossom has brought great joy to Kristen. As opposed to the brittle, timid dog he once was, Wally now adores being in the spotlight. He considers himself the boss of his doggy siblings, Lily and Cooper, as well as the occasional fosters.

He has a bit of a cheeky side and has even been known to steal toys from Lily and sit on them so she cannot retrieve them.

Wally's favorite activity is running fearlessly through snow. He loves partaking in adventures, such as accompanying Kristen to dog-friendly spots around town and even travelling with her to destinations like New York City. An innately fashionable pup, he also likes wearing doggy clothes such as sweaters and bandanas.

Kristen documents his adventures and photogenic personality through his Instagram account, which has served as a beacon of light for folks across the globe. People have been inspired by Wally's story and how he owns his look—especially his tongue-filled smile—with pride. One of his photos was even reposted by Ellen DeGeneres with the caption, "This dog could absolutely be my best friend."

Despite all the fame his new chapter has brought, Wally is still first and foremost a mama's boy. While the common term for stories such as theirs is "foster fail," for Kristen and Wally, their relationship is more accurately characterized as a "foster success!"

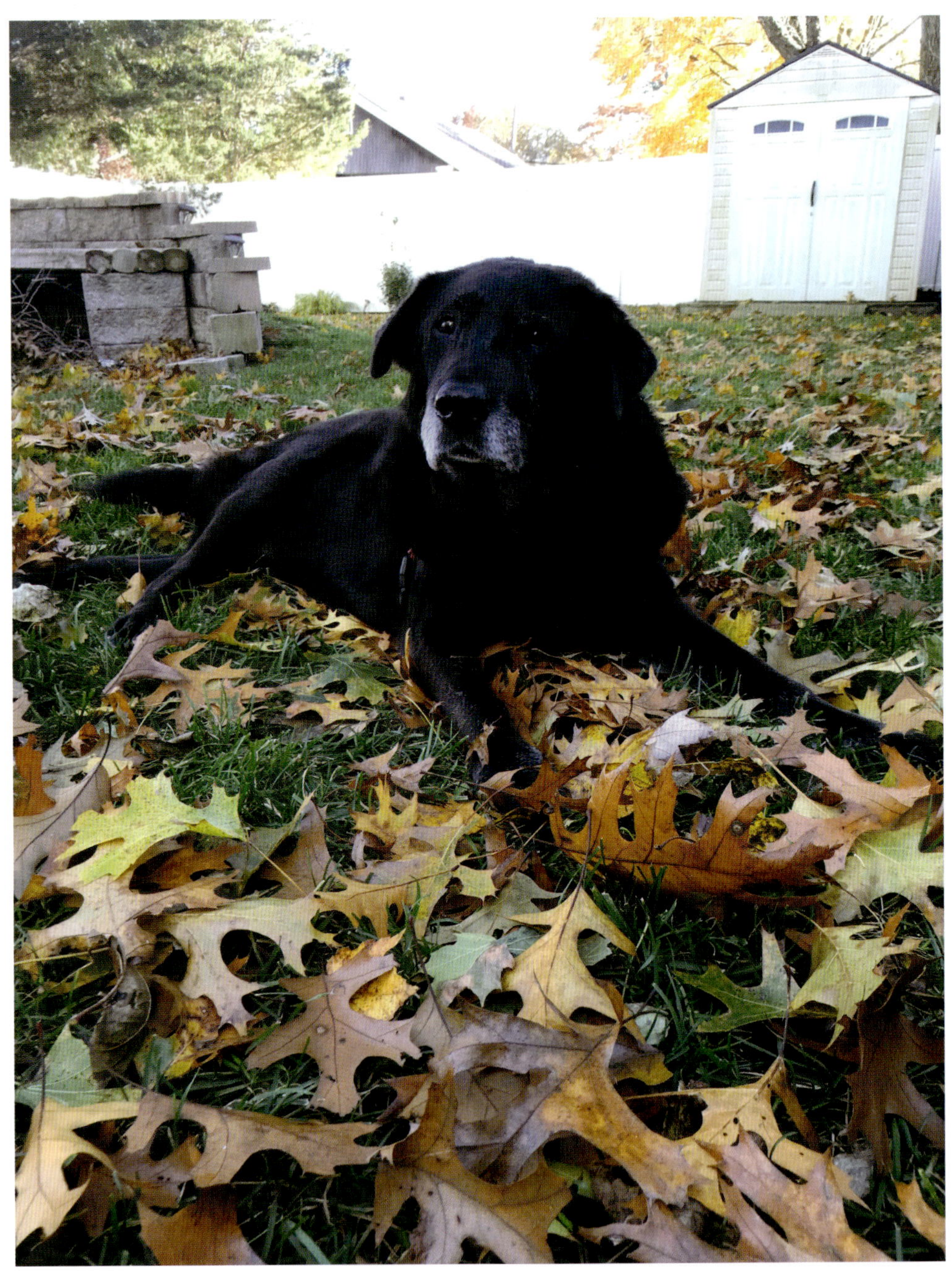

BEAR, 17

Before finding his forever home, Bear spent fifteen long, painful years tethered to a tree and weighed down by a thirty-five-pound chain. His previous owners intended for him to serve them as a guard dog, and sadly, in return for his service, they never allowed him to set one paw inside their home. It was a solitary life for Bear, but fortunately his story did not end there; in fact, it was far from over.

Bear finally felt compassion when a rescue group known as the Guardians of Rescue convinced his owners to release him into their care. They filmed his official unchaining, and the footage captured hearts across the world, which subsequently spiraled Bear into cyber fame. He was transported to the Save-A-Pet adoption agency, which searched to find him the perfect, everlasting home he deserved.

Kerrie of New York was also looking for a fresh start and a new chapter. She had recently endured a divorce and suffered the devastating passing of her black lab, Zack. Her morning routine did not typically include turning on the television, but something inside compelled her to turn on *Good Morning America* one morning. It just so happened they were airing a feature on none other than Bear with the hope of landing him his forever home. Bear stole the show, quite literally; Ricky Gervais pivoted attention to Bear throughout a segment which was originally intended to promote Ricky's new movie.

Kerrie felt an instant connection with Bear through her television screen, and his story tugged at her innermost heartstrings. Bear reminded her of Zack, who had shown her that senior dogs offered a love that is pure, unconditional, honest, sweet, and gentle. However, Kerrie was far from the only person who felt a devotion to Bear that day; in fact, the rescue received hundreds, if not thousands, of applications. After careful review of said applications, they determined Kerrie was the perfect fit for Bear. Luckily for Bear, the rescue got this decision right, and his new chapter would become his best yet.

Kerrie understood that adopting a senior dog would likely come with a level of heartbreak, especially since Bear was already fifteen years old. While she did not know how much time she would have with Bear, Kerrie was certain she could provide Bear with a forever home full of love, which is an emotion he had not experienced nor received before.

Despite years of living outside, Bear adjusted to his indoor lifestyle quite nicely. He and Kerrie embraced each other and commenced their new chapters together. Now, at a remarkable seventeen years old, Bear likes to walk around his backyard with Kerrie right next to him at every step. At times, he will fall down or walk into things as a result of aging, but Kerrie always makes sure to pick him up and steer him in the right direction. While his gait has slowed, his spirit and outlook certainly have not.

Just by looking at him, it is possible you would never suspect Bear had ever been anything but an indoor dog. He loves to eat, and he especially relishes salmon treats, a flavor he likely never tasted in his early years. Bear is known for flashing an irresistible "Elvis" smile, in which half of his lip curls up adorably like the king himself. Bear has also mastered the perfect "cute" face by staring up lovingly with one ear up, while his other ear turns downwards.

Kerrie chronicles Bear's new chapter through his Instagram account, and people around the world have been touched by his story. He has also earned his infamous nickname, "Goodest Bear."

Although Bear has endured some physical battles throughout his new chapter, including two separate bouts of vestibular disease, his inner fighter spirit has remained unbroken. He continues to live out his new chapter unchained, both physically and metaphorically.

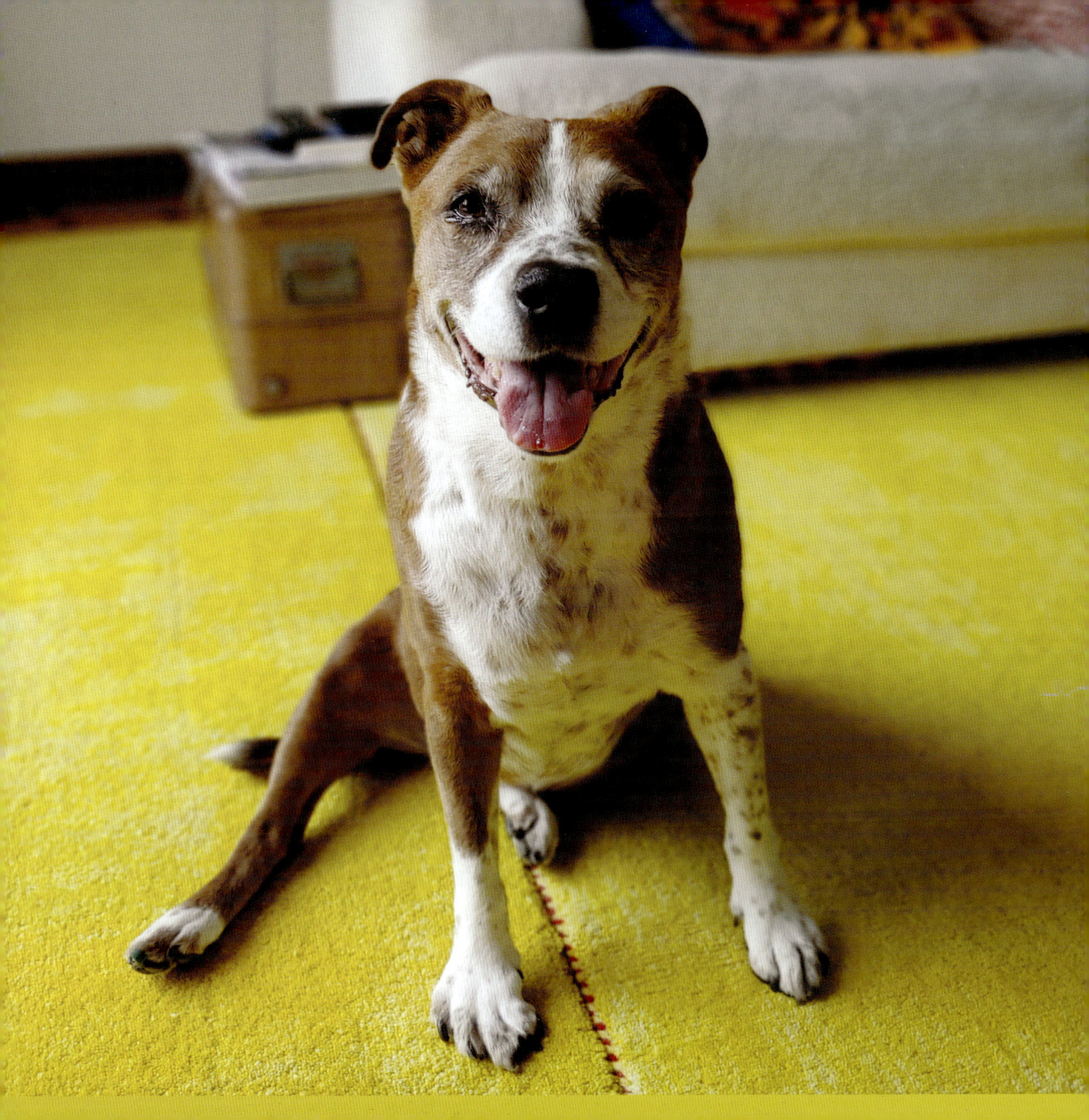

DOROTHY, 11

Dorothy is known for her irresistible grin, but sadly, the origins of her adoption story were nothing to smile about. At eight years old and with a mammary tumor, Dorothy was surrendered by her former owner at the Sacramento County Bradshaw Animal Shelter. In spite of her advanced age and illness, the shelter offered her a second chance, likely because of her undeniable charm. Soon thereafter, surgeons successfully removed her tumor, and Dorothy was given the opportunity to peacefully recover at the home of a foster mom named Gwen.

That same year, married couple Anne and Chris of San Francisco, California began searching for a dog to join their family. Although Chris had prior dog ownership experience, it was an entirely new adventure for Anne, who had never before had a canine family member. As firm believers in second chances, the couple made the conscious decision to seek an older dog, since they are often the dogs most in need of second chances.

Anne stumbled across Dorothy on Petfinder in a "you may also like" side search bar on the website. In her adoption profile photograph, Dorothy was flashing her best smile beneath a flower crown. It was so awe-inspiring that, even after facing immense adversity, Dorothy upheld her positivity. Her resilience spoke to Anne and Chris, and in their hearts, they knew she was the one.

The couple travelled over an hour and a half to meet Dorothy in Sacramento. As they visited with her, they were delighted to watch as Dorothy brought to life the personality from her photo. The three went for a walk together, during which Dorothy led the way while also continuously looking back over her shoulder with a lovable grin. At the end of the walk, Anne asked Dorothy if she would like to return to San Francisco with them. Almost too perfectly, Dorothy responded with placing her front paws on Anne's shoulders and presenting her with a doggy kiss. It was then, roughly eight months after being deserted by her former family, that this lovable eight-year-old dog had finally found her forever home.

Dorothy transitioned to San Francisco life quite smoothly, and her personality blossomed further as she became comfortable in her new surroundings. Anne and Chris soon discovered that Dorothy is a super expressive dog, and her smile is her trademark look. Much to their amusement, Dorothy quickly began communicating with them using a series of snorting sounds, which they consider her own special language. Dorothy also has learned a new human language, Dutch, as Anne is from the Netherlands and frequently speaks in her mother tongue.

Dorothy's personality is innately social and friendly. In their early days together when the three were living in an area near many public transportation hubs, Dorothy would greet all the commuters she passed. Flash forward three years, and Anne and Chris now lovingly admit that Dorothy, now eleven years old, has more human friends than they do.

Through a canine DNA test, it was discovered that Dorothy is a mixture of Australian cattle dog, pit bull, and beagle. This unique breeding combination is very telling of her behaviors and tendencies. Her cattle dog pedigree shines as she is keen on herding all her human friends into the same room, especially if that room is near the snacks. The beagle in her often emerges when she is feeling like a detective. She likes to solve mysteries, such as where the neighborhood skunks like to lurk. Once she solves the mystery, she always treats the skunks, and all living things, with the utmost respect while displaying her pit bull lineage.

When Dorothy is feeling her best, her inner puppy will surface in the form of the "zoomies" or a horse-like gallop. She has enjoyed many hikes at places like the old quarry in Pacifica, but as she has continued to age, she typically requires a day of rest and recovery afterward. Dorothy's hind legs are not as strong as they once were, but luckily, she has two parents who ensure she gets the best possible care. Chris regularly takes her to acupuncture and hydrotherapy appointments at A Well Adjusted Pet in San Francisco.

While Dorothy has many beds available throughout the entire house, her favorite resting spot is always the one closest to Anne and Chris. She can often be found sprawled out by their feet as they work at their desks. It is safe to say that moments such as these in Dorothy's new chapter are certainly worthy of her infamous smile!

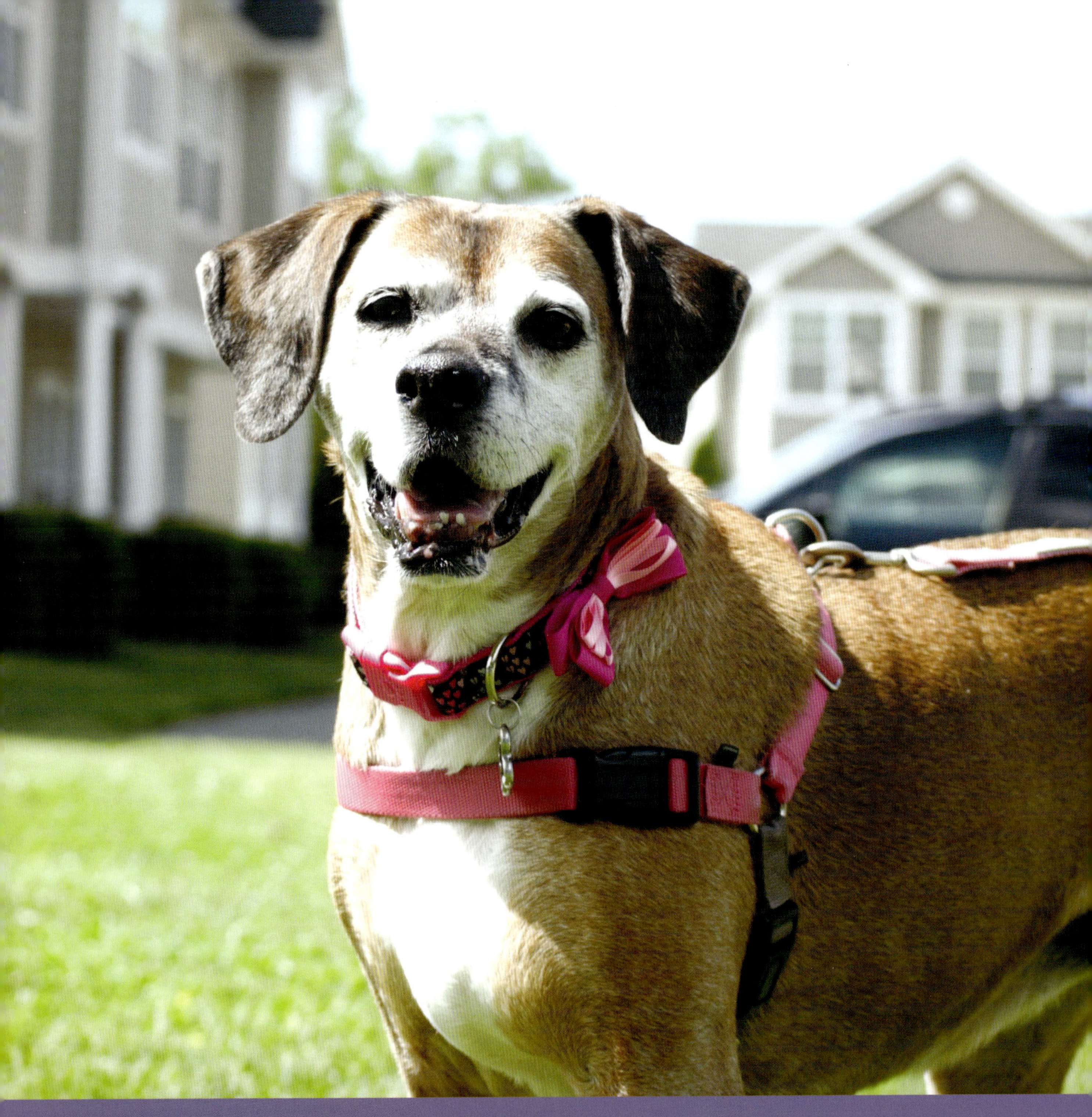

KHALEESI, 10

Just like her television namesake, Khaleesi, the senior boxer rescue, is both brave and resilient. She was faced with adversity at an elderly age when her military owner was relocated and could no longer care for her. Upon hearing of Khaleesi's looming homelessness, a neighbor graciously agreed to take her in temporarily. While this new living situation was impermanent and primarily an outdoor offering, it helped Khaleesi avoid enduring the dreadful alternative of the local kill shelter.

An animal loving gentleman named Lee came to cherish Khaleesi and worked to network her story through social media in the hopes of landing her a forever home. Every day, he visited Khaleesi and showered her with affection. He also accompanied her on long strolls around the neighborhood, which were the highlight of her day.

Christi from Virginia is no stranger to helping animals in need. For more than three years, she has continually supported animal rescue organizations and even fostered homeless pets. When Christi stumbled upon Lee's Facebook post pleading for a home for an elderly boxer, her heart broke as she scrolled through the photos of sad-eyed, elderly Khaleesi, who was just looking for a peaceful retirement home and family to call her own.

After six weeks of viewing the reoccurring posts, Christi and her husband, Chris, ultimately agreed to open their home to foster Khaleesi indoors until a permanent owner could be found. When they brought Khaleesi home, they were distraught when Khaleesi's first action was to run away. It crushed them to know Khaleesi was unable to comprehend they were just trying to offer her a loving home. After a panic-filled ten minutes, Christi and Chris were relieved to finally track Khaleesi down.

Khaleesi's initial worries and reservations soon dissolved as she began trusting her new family. She quickly evolved from rarely wagging her tail to being so outwardly happy that she wiggled her whole butt constantly. Christi and her family fell head over heels in love with Khaleesi within one week. Their initial plan of merely serving as a foster was thrown out the door, and they quickly made Khaleesi a permanent member of her family through officially adopting her. Luckily, the feelings were mutual, as Khaleesi equally adored her new family, including her human brother, Tristen, and fellow rescue pup, Reggie.

Khaleesi soon readjusted to indoor life and recognized her new residence has several unfamiliar privileges, some of which were quite confusing to Khaleesi initially. For example, the concept of being allowed on a human bed was completely foreign to Khaleesi. Christi had to physically teach Khaleesi how to jump on a bed. Now, Khaleesi puts herself to bed, and her family often finds her sound asleep, typically exuding boisterous, yet adorable snores.

Khaleesi appreciates her time outdoors, likely because she has recognized it will always end with her being welcomed back inside. She can often be found basking in the sun's rays while positioned in a frog-like pose. As with many dogs, her favorite activity is going on walks. Whenever Christi utters "bye-bye" or motions towards a leash, Khaleesi dances in pure excitement as she anticipates the adventure that lies ahead. She walks at a slowed pace, and her daily walk rituals include stopping to sniff each smell she encounters. Khaleesi also likes to bark at any geese that are foolish enough to stand in her path.

Khaleesi has formed a special bond with her doggy brother, Reggie, with whom she shares a rescue background. To her family's amusement, Khaleesi often mimics Reggie's behaviors and tendencies. If Reggie barks, you can expect that Khaleesi will also. She has even been known to be protective of him at the dog park.

As Khaleesi has eased into her new life and family, she has not forgotten her friend, Lee, who still comes to visit her regularly. Each time Lee arrives, she flashes a lovable smile and wiggles her butt at a hyperactive speed. It is almost as if she is saying, "Thank you, I'll never forget what you did for me."

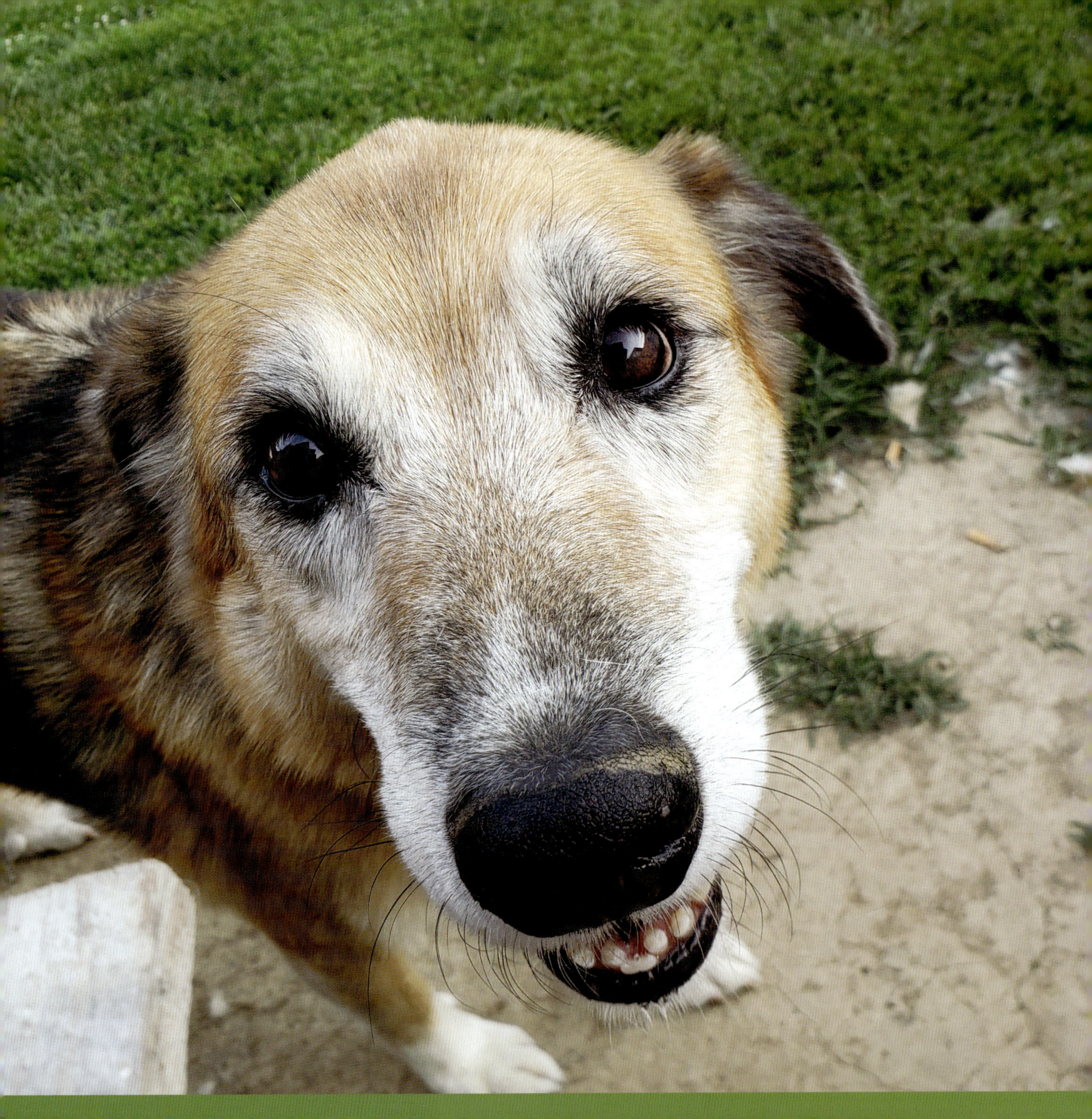

SCOOBY, 13

Scooby's multi-state journey began in Texas, where he miraculously survived a year in a kill shelter after being found as a stray senior. In addition to the uneasiness brought about from his new surroundings, Scooby also had to endure a painful paw injury that was left untreated. Scooby later was transferred to the no-kill Delaware Humane Association.

Although the change in scenery was a pleasant change of pace, Scooby was still extremely reserved and spent most of his time curled up on the largest bed he could find. He was interested in the other shelter dogs, but he was not too keen on actually playing with them; he had bigger things on his mind, like finding his forever home.

Jackee of Delaware was a consistent savior to animals in need, and she frequently opened her home to foster homeless dogs. One of her beloved fosters was Gracie, a senior boxer who was malnourished, suffering from cancer, and only expected to live a few weeks. With Jackee's constant affection and superior care, Gracie survived for three months surrounded by love before passing away. While saying a final goodbye to Gracie was heartbreaking for Jackee, the experience was also enlightening; it showed her the good that can come from offering a second chance to a senior rescue dog.

Jackee had been working at the Delaware Humane Society for more than three years when Scooby arrived. She surely was not actively searching for a new dog, but something in Scooby's eyes tugged at her heartstrings. Scooby had been passed over many times because of his senior age and large build—not to mention, he was also almost fully deaf.

For Jackee, these traits only enhanced her readiness to adopt him. Although she was already a mother to six other rescue dogs, Jackee was prepared to provide him with the means to live a happy life, no matter how long that might be.

After he arrived at his new home, Scooby's behavior initially mirrored the way he acted in the shelter. He isolated himself from his new doggy siblings and spent most of his time sleeping in his bed. When he was awake, he was mostly silent. He did not run to greet Jackee when she arrived home like the other dogs, and he even required excessive coaxing just to go outside.

Jackee recognized Scooby had been through quite a lot and would need time to feel comfortable, so she and her other dogs gave him the space to settle in on his own terms. About two months later, Scooby decided it was finally time to speak up, and he let out a thunderous bark out of nowhere. It was a bark heard around the world, and it was Scooby's way of saying, "Hey, I'm here and ready to play!" The bark was so startling to his new doggy brothers and sisters, that they initially just stared at him with deep looks of confusion.

That first bark served as a turning point for Scooby; from then onward, he was a content member of the family and doggy pack. He is no longer fearful of speaking up, and he now frequently barks as a means to tell Jackee when he wants something. While he gets along with all his new family members, he has formed an exceptional bond with his sister, Letty, a three-year-old boxer/shepherd mix. Now, when Letty moves, Scooby is always close behind.

Since embracing his new chapter, Scooby feels comfort in being outside, no matter the weather conditions Mother Nature offers. He also likes to be pampered and often embodies a Fabio-type personality while being brushed. In fact, he will stand indefinitely with his head perked up if it means he can be brushed. After years on the streets and shelter, it is no surprise that he takes pleasure in finally maintaining nice hair.

Scooby now goes by many names, such as Scoobs, Doobs, and Bugs, but no matter what, his favorite identity is as a proud member of his new pack!

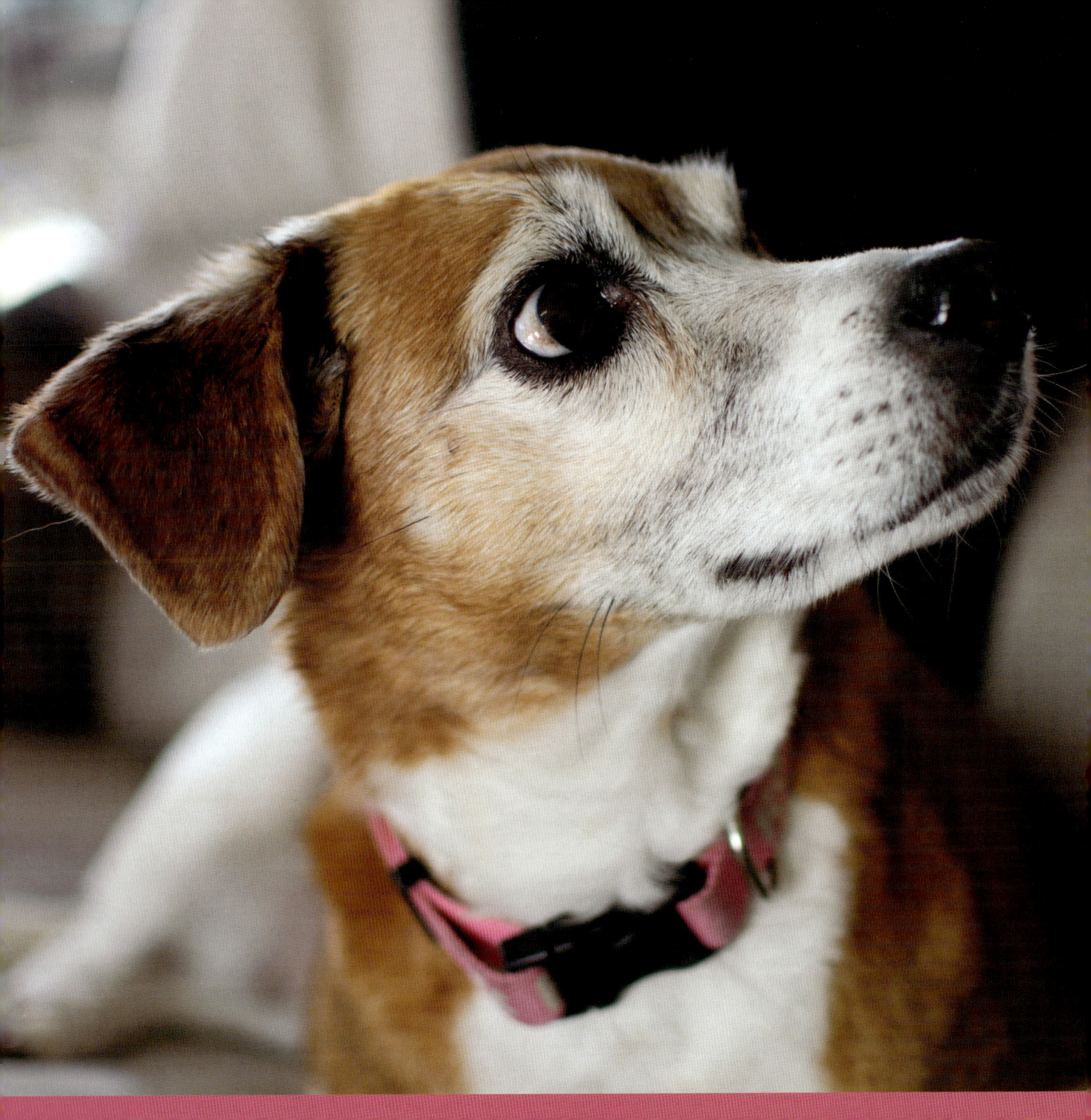

ROSIE, 13

"Kill" is never a pleasant word, but it is especially bad when it is followed by the word "shelter." At eleven years old, a sweet hound mix named Rosie found herself in such a place. Fortunately, she escaped the dreadful, often-impending fate of a kill shelter when she was transferred to the Lynchburg Humane Society (LHS). While it is uncertain exactly how long she was held at the kill shelter, it is undeniable that her transfer served as a lifeline for dodging a tragic outcome.

Life at LHS was far better for Rosie, but she exhibited signs of confusion and anxiety while desiring a home of her own. She had a history of Lyme disease, and a combination of both stress and skin allergies caused her legs to become pink and hairless. She was not exactly the most sought-after adoption candidate, especially with her elderly age, so she remained at the shelter for many months. Things looked up for Rosie momentarily when one family adopted her, but that good fortune was short-lived as the family quickly returned her to LHS after indicating she did not do well with children.

Although they were avid animal supporters, married couple Thaddee and Katherine of Virginia had no plans to adopt a dog. In fact, they had never owned a dog before. One weekend, Katherine volunteered in the cat unit at LHS while Thaddee poked around the building and peered at some of the dogs. He came across pitiful, morose Rosie sitting in her own enclosure in a room designated for puppies. Thaddee felt immediate sympathy, so he persuaded Katherine to come take a look. After seeing Rosie's condition, Katherine also felt instant empathy. Because dog adoption was not in their forecasted plans and they were inexperienced with canine ownership, the couple left the shelter that day without Rosie.

In the subsequent weeks, Thaddee and Katherine could not erase images of Rosie from their thoughts. Katherine continued to volunteer in the cat ward of LHS, and she always made sure to make a stop to check on Rosie. Each visit, Katherine discovered Rosie in the same enclosure with a look of depression as her head sat atop her paws. All the puppies around her were being adopted, while Rosie sat isolated and in despair.

After a few visits and countless fluttering thoughts, Thaddee and Katherine decided enough was enough, so they agreed to meet Rosie up close and not just through the glass of her enclosure. Something about her stole their hearts, and they felt compelled to adopt her as they held her lovingly. Being that Rosie was an older, house-trained, less energetic dog, the couple figured she would serve as an ideal way to transition into dog ownership. They put their application in and officially welcomed her into their homes the next day; alas, Rosie's nine-month residency at LHS was over!

Thaddee and Katherine soon realized that despite her senior status, Rosie still had energy left. Initially, she did not seem to understand how to play. The couple tried giving her toys, but she was confused about exactly what they wanted her to do with them. Her enthusiasm for toys has since evolved, and she now loves to sniff out treats from puzzle-type toys. Presently, at thirteen years old, Rosie still has energy left and even likes to join her parents on hikes.

Throughout their time with Rosie, Thaddee and Katherine have learned that even though Rosie was let down by humans in the past, she is still very loving and trusting of all people. Although she was previously tagged as being "bad with children," they have only seen her exude calmness and patience when interacting with children.

Rosie spends many of her days accompanying Katherine to work, during which she mostly naps peacefully on a blanket in the office. Rosie's presence serves as a beacon of serenity in the office, especially during stressful periods. Many of Katherine's colleagues even refer to her as the unofficial office therapy dog.

Over the course of their relationship, Rosie has taught her parents how to be dog owners, and they, in return, have taught her how to be a dog. Thaddee and Katherine say that more than anything, their personalities have changed in the two years Rosie has been a part of their family. Initially, they implemented many rules, such as: no dog on the sofa, no dog on the bed, and no dog in the bedroom at all. Their rulebook was reversed completely over time; now, Rosie sits wherever she desires, and the only household rule is, "Don't disturb Rosie!"

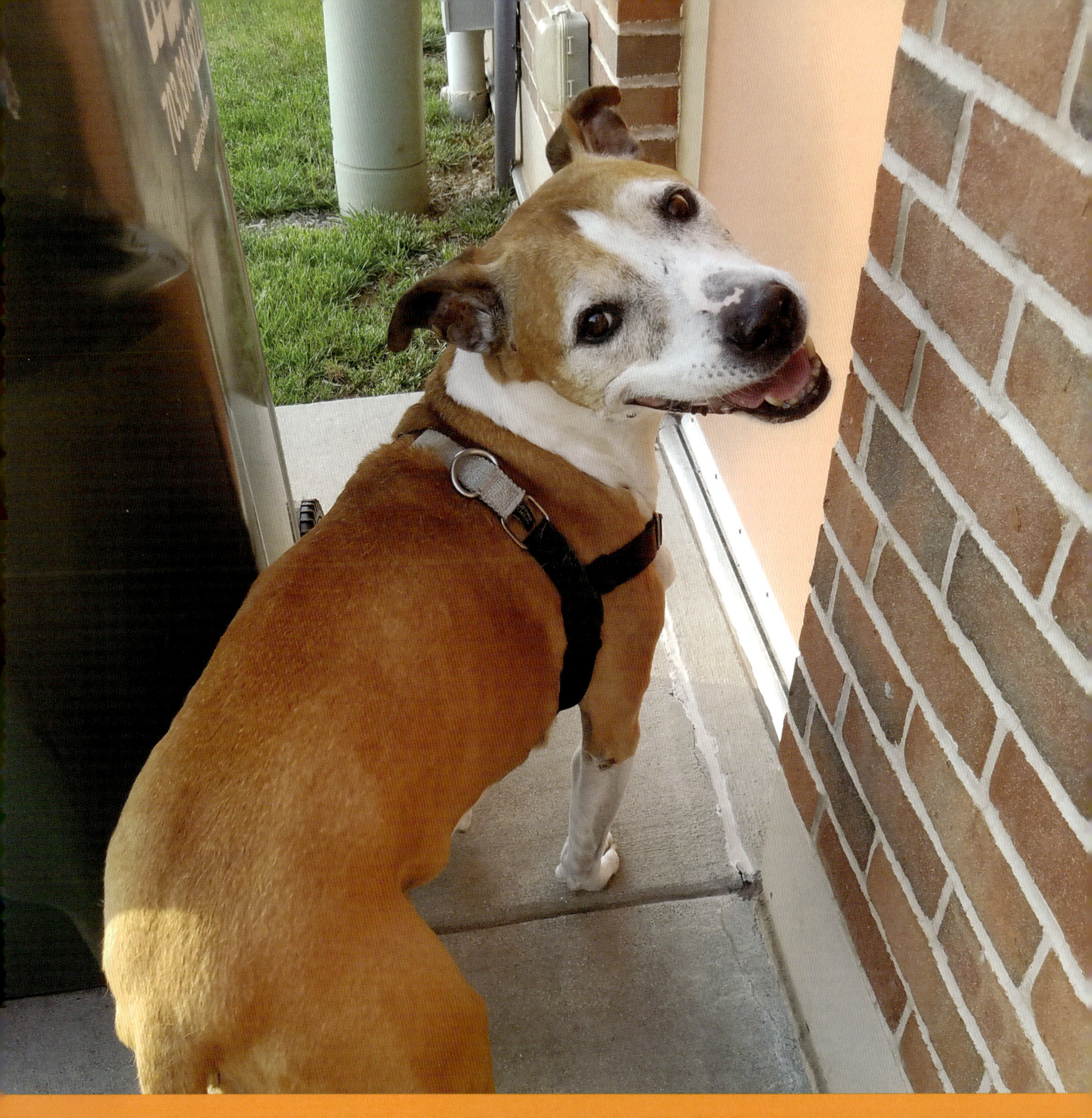

HOPPER, 14

Hopper's name is a slight indication of his unstable past. Throughout his tumultuous former years, he "hopped" around without landing on a permanent home. His story originated when he was found as a stray puppy in 2004. Because he was a charming young pup, it was no surprise he was adopted quickly. It was a surprise, however, when his first family expanded a few years later with the arrival of a newborn, and subsequently decided they could no longer care for Hopper.

Ultimately, they dropped him off at the same rescue organization that had originally taken him in, the Friends of Homeless Animals (FOHA). The adoption experience was far less positive for Hopper the next time around, as he was no longer a sought-after puppy. He ended up bearing a ten-year stint in the shelter, with a few intermittent foster care stays while dealing with illness.

Throughout those long ten years, the shelter took great care of Hopper and networked him heavily on social media in the hopes that the right person would come along. Being that he was a pit bull with dog aggressive tendencies and health issues, the odds were certainly stacked against him, and the years began to pass. As Hopper got older, his chances of adoption decreased. Despite the obstacles, the shelter did not give up hope, and neither did Hopper.

In late summer of 2018, Delfina of Virginia suffered the agonizing loss of her first dog, Riley. She initially anticipated it would be a while before she could muster the strength to bring another dog into her home, but after about a month, she slowly started following various animal rescue organizations on social media. She soon came across a tear-jerking Instagram post for a dog who had been at the shelter for far too long. That dog—you guessed it—was Hopper.

As she read Hopper's story, Delfina was reminded of Riley, as both dogs were pit bulls found as strays and were considered to be dog aggressive. It crushed her to know how many years Hopper had spent in a shelter, and she was dead-set on refusing to let him finish out his life there. She commented on the post to let the rescue shelter know she had every intention of adopting Hopper, as long as they agreed she was a good fit.

The following weekend, Delfina drove her mother and niece to meet him at the shelter. The in-person connection was also instantaneous, as Hopper again reminded Delfina of her beloved Riley. She could not bear the thought of him spending any more time at the shelter. With the support of her mother and niece, she brought Hopper home exactly two months after Riley's passing.

Although he had only spent very limited time in a home setting throughout the previous years, Hopper became accustomed to his new life rather quickly. Somewhere during the transition, his name took on a new meaning as he formed a new lease on life in Delfina's care; he now hops in excitement and wags his tail constantly!

He continually stares out the window, as if to soak in the big world he could not witness throughout his time at the shelter. Fittingly, he adores his walks, during which he loves to explore the outdoors while always expressing a deep look of intent. Delfina has learned he always appears to be on a mission. Despite having a stocky figure, Hopper is quite clumsy. While his adorable tumbles are often a source of laughter, Delfina finds herself ever-repeating, "Be careful, Hopper!"

Delfina has picked up on some of Hopper's funny mannerisms and traits, like getting the "zoomies" whenever he becomes wet, and occasionally eating a potato if one is offered to him. He also likes playing tug of war with rope toys, probably because he has realized how much fun he can have with someone on the other side of the toy.

Despite all the play and kookiness, Hopper is mostly a silent dog and almost never makes a peep. This is likely because he appreciates the quiet serenity of his new home after tolerating so many years of boisterous sounds at the shelter. He is not an avid cuddler; however, Delfina has noticed he has slowly started to come around and embrace her cuddle attempts, especially in the mornings after breakfast.

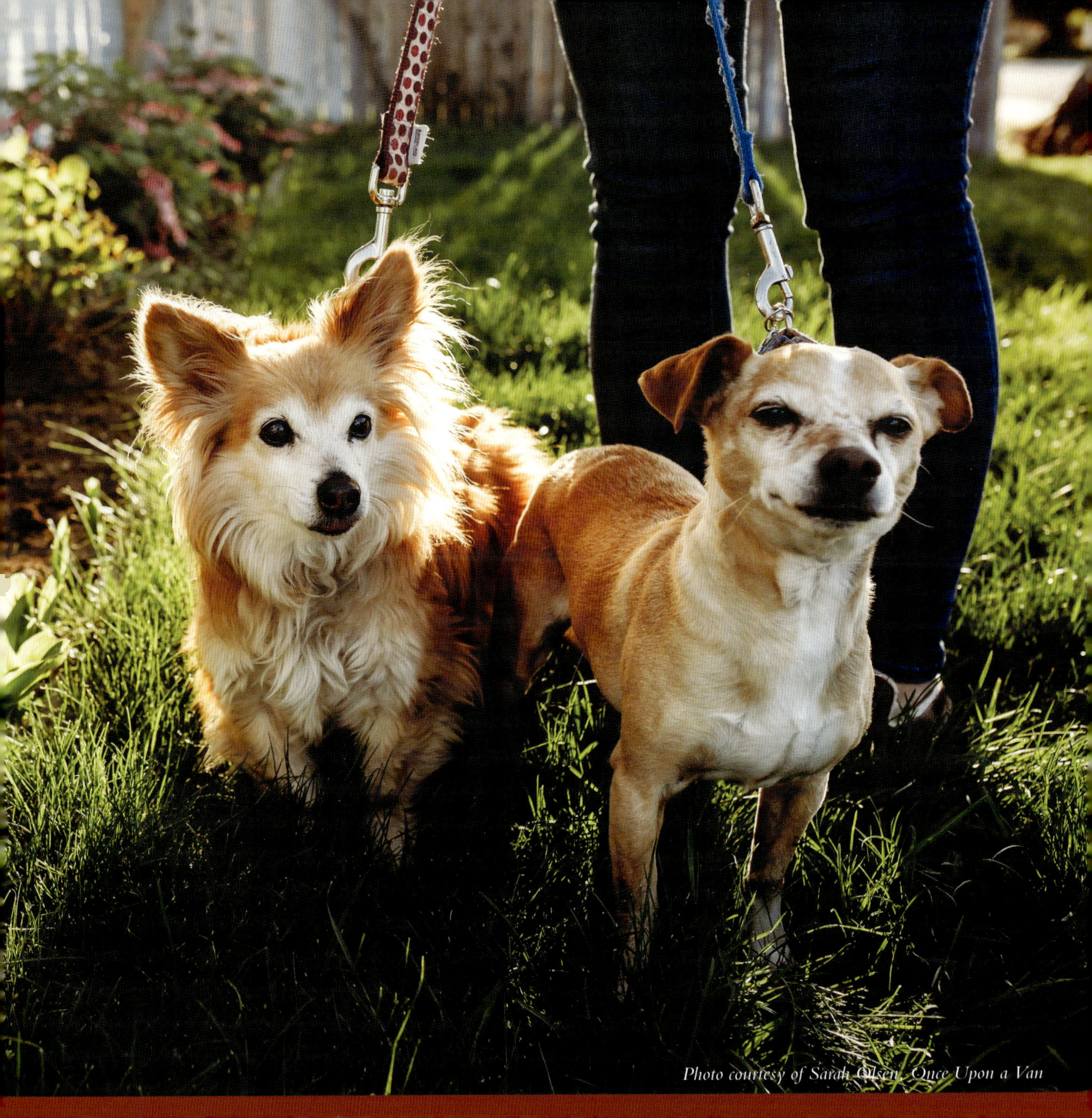

Photo courtesy of Sarah Olsen, Once Upon a Van

GANDALF, 14; AND OATEY, 10

While they were living in Seattle, married couple Nathan and Ashley yearned for a canine companion. Their professions demanded extended work hours, so they recognized it was not the right time to add a dog into their hectic schedules. Eventually, Nathan began a new job at a company with a dog-friendly office. With this favorable news, the couple actively searched for an older rescue dog with special needs to join their family. They hated the idea of animals being abandoned, especially animals who were less likely to be adopted due to their age or condition.

Nathan and Ashley discovered Gandalf, a petite thirteen-year-old dog, through Seattle Humane's foster program. Not much was known about Gandalf's past, except that he was found as a stray in Yakima, Washington one year prior. When originally taken in, Gandalf was not neutered and had dreadlocks infested with fleas, giardia, and severe dental problems. Fortunately, he was found by good Samaritans who ensured he was fixed up both medically and aesthetically.

The couple went to meet Gandalf the day they saw his online profile. For them, it was love at first sight during the initial interaction; for Gandalf, the connection took longer. His foster mom, Evelyn, indicated that many people had expressed interest in adopting him, but they were put off by his standoffish temperament. According to Nathan and Ashley, Gandalf's aloofness only added to their desire to adopt him. They recognized they could offer him a chance to come out of his shell on his own terms and really be himself in his senior years.

Gandalf revealed his personality as he became comfortable in his new surroundings. Nathan and Ashley have determined that, like his literary namesake, Gandalf is an old wizard with many quirks and layers. He has some physical disabilities, since he is deaf and mostly blind, but these shortcomings certainly do not keep him from enjoying his retirement years. He savors his time outdoors and—much to his parents' surprise—he is an avid swimmer when placed in shallow open water. Initially, he did not care to be touched, but he has since developed an attachment to his new parents and now accepts their attention. He will even rest indefinitely for a good chin rub.

In the early days of their family of three, Nathan's daily routine included a three-mile roundtrip commute to his job in Seattle, which was more than Gandalf's old legs could handle. To make things easier for them both, Nathan pushed Gandalf in a stroller after the first half-mile. Nathan stands tall at six feet, four inches and maintains a burly physique, so seeing him pushing a miniature, geriatric dog in a stroller was quite a sight to behold for onlookers in downtown Seattle.

Eventually, Nathan and Ashley uprooted and moved to Boise, Idaho. One of the advantages of their relocation was a larger house with a yard, meaning the couple now had room to add another dog to their family. Because of their positive relationship and experience with Gandalf, the couple knew they again wanted to adopt a senior rescue. They stumbled upon ten-year-old Oatey through Petango at All Valley Animal Care Center.

They learned Oatey once had a family, but was sadly surrendered at seven years old. He was subsequently adopted for three years, but was again returned because the family's other dogs were bullying Oatey, which resulted in scars covering his head and muzzle.

Unlike Gandalf, Oatey was outwardly affectionate during their introduction. Immediately, he wanted to cuddle and play fetch. Even though he was ten years old, Oatey was a ball of energy. Nathan and Ashley quickly determined Oatey was a perfect addition to their family. Because of Gandalf's calm nature, they were confident Oatey was no longer at risk for bullying.

Since welcoming him to their home, Oatey has been persistent about playing with Gandalf, but Gandalf's response is often to waddle away from Oatey's sometimes overwhelming energy. When Gandalf denies his attempts to play, Oatey often turns his attention to his favorite squeaky raccoon toy. He also intervenes whenever the family cats get into a tussle, perhaps because it reminds him of the altercations he endured in his previous household.

Nathan and Ashley have enjoyed witnessing their two dogs' relationship evolve and how Gandalf has grown with Oatey's presence. Because of Oatey, Gandalf has continued to learn to accept love and find his inner confidence. He has started to embrace his little sibling's energetic personality, and now the two can sometimes even be found cuddling.

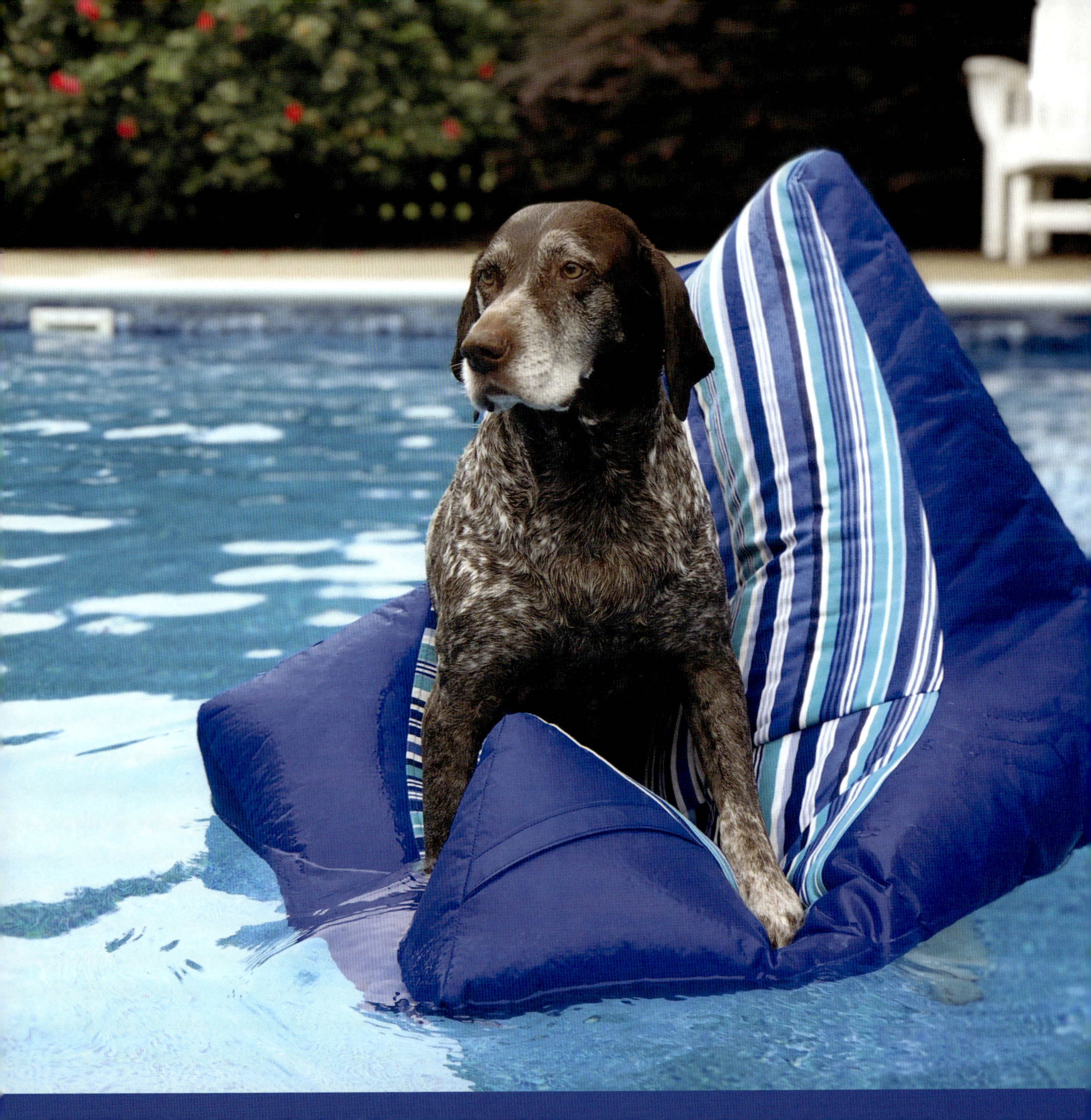

GERTIE, 9

After she spent eight years with her beloved family, Gertie's owners filed for divorce. As their divorce proceedings were carried out, each party indicated they would no longer be equipped to care for Gertie. As Gertie's future remained unknown, her owners reached out to the Mid-Atlantic German Shorthaired Pointer (GSP) Rescue for assistance in finding her a new home.

Lori and Bill of Virginia were already the proud owners of a three-year-old GSP named Remi. They were also parents to four adult human children but had recently become empty nesters. Realizing they had more free time on their hands, Lori and Bill decided they wanted to take in another GSP.

Throughout their twenty-eight-year marriage, Lori and Bill had been longtime owners of several GSPs and were quite familiar with the breed. Lori had recently begun following the Mid-Atlantic GSP Rescue on Facebook, and she soon noticed a posting about Gertie needing a new home. She was immediately interested in adopting Gertie, and her heart broke as she read Gertie's situation.

Adopting an older dog was a new venture for Lori and Bill, so they carefully deliberated before deciding to fill out an application for Gertie. Ultimately, they concluded it did not matter how much time Gertie had left; what mattered most was their ability to offer her the loving home she deserved during her golden years.

After a thorough home check, the rescue representatives quickly determined that Lori and Bill were the best adoption candidates for Gertie. After all, they were familiar with the breed, and they had a spacious fenced-in backyard and a pool which they allowed their dogs to swim in freely. Plus, the rescue predicted Remi's companionship might ease Gertie's transition into her new life.

The initial adoption experience was not quite as straightforward as Lori and Bill expected, and they were forced to face some rather difficult hurdles from the get-go. When they went to officially pick up Gertie, they noticed a large tumor in her eye. They were concerned, but never thought twice about canceling the adoption over something Gertie had no control over.

With the rescue's full support, they immediately took her to a vet. They were then referred over to a canine eye specialist—a veterinary field of which they were not aware even existed. The diagnosis was tragic; Gertie had eye cancer. Through a complex surgery, the eye specialist successfully removed the entire tumor without having to extract her eye. Gertie was officially a cancer survivor, and Bill and Lori were thrilled they were able to get her the care she needed.

On top of her eye complications, Gertie moaned incessantly during the initial weeks in her new home. Lori and Bill tried everything they could think of to make her feel comfortable around them and in their home, but her moaning continued. Adding to the chaos, Gertie was not fond of Remi at first. Specifically, she did not appreciate Remi's playful personality.

After a few weeks, Gertie came to the realization that her new home was not all that dreadful. In fact, it is a dog retirement paradise. She had been used to spending more than half the day in a crate in her old home, but she is now given free rein in her new home.

She also enjoys a massive backyard where she can run wild and sniff as much as she pleases. At first, she was timid about entering the pool. Now, one of her favorite activities is to bask atop a pool float for extended periods of time, conveying her innermost Cleopatra. The adventures do not stop there, for she also regularly goes on hikes and long walks.

As Gertie relishes the amenities of her new residence, she also fully embraces Lori, Bill, and Remi. Now, she shadows them wherever they go. Although she weighs more than sixty pounds, she wholeheartedly believes she is a lap dog. She has been known to casually put her full bodyweight on Lori and Bill just to ensure she is as close to them as possible. She also will often choose to share a dog bed with Remi, instead of resting in her own.

Even though Gertie's adoption story began tragically as the result of a divorce, she has grown content with her new family and their lifestyle. Surrounded by endless love and fun, she certainly has nothing to moan about anymore!

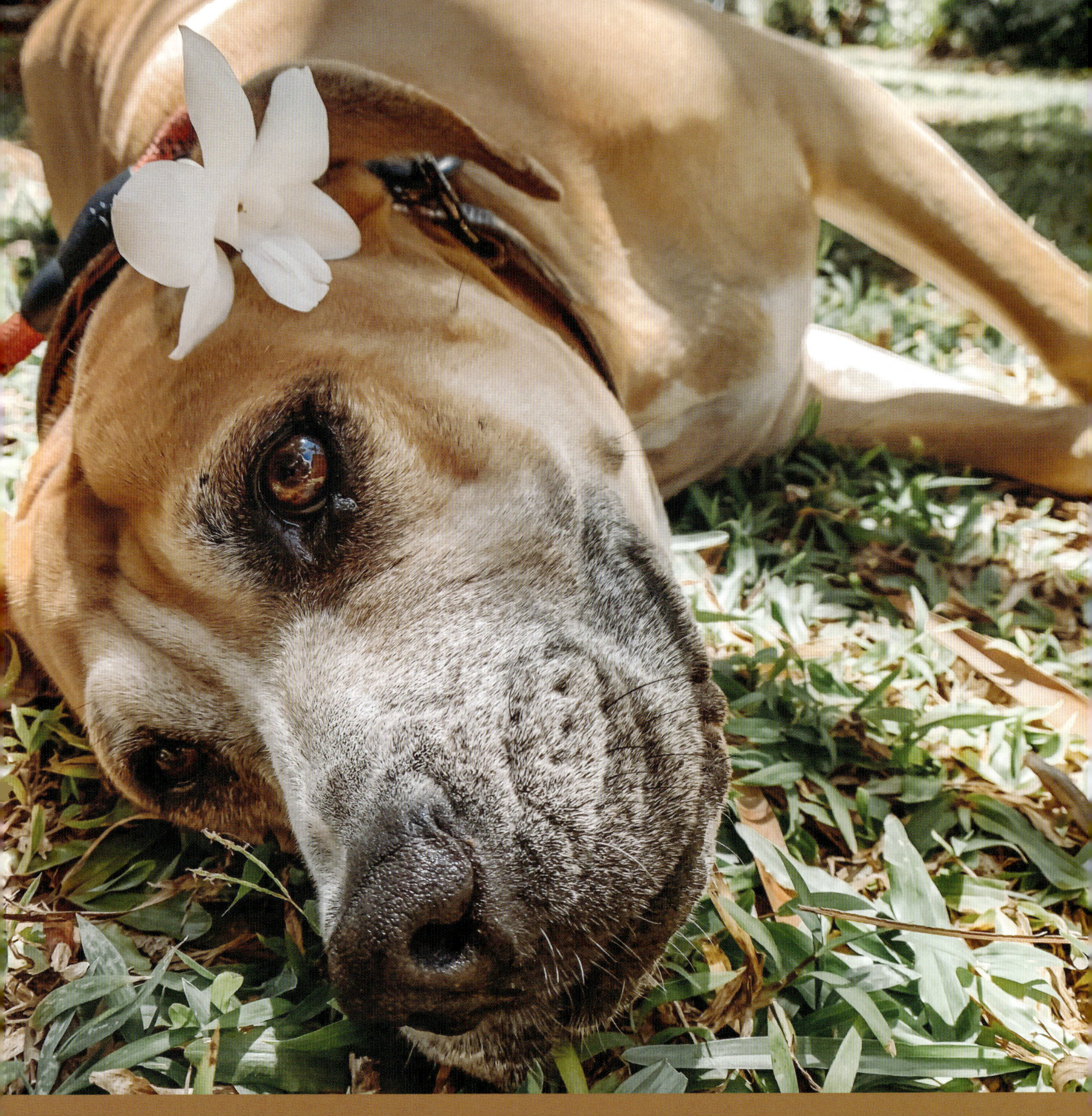

DREAMY, 10

When Dreamy was found on the side of the road and taken in by the Kauai Humane Society, little was known about her backstory. From the physical clues on her body, it was clear she had been a mother, and maybe even used repeatedly for breeding, at some point in her past.

Natalie of Hawaii had not owned a dog since childhood and, admittedly, she was not entirely confident she was even a dog person. One day, she and her boyfriend, Ian, felt compelled to make a stop at the Kauai Humane Society. They were curious about the dogs but did not anticipate they would end up taking one home with them that day.

As they walked through the shelter, they peered at the adoptable dogs and stopped by one dog that was roughly five years old. After a meet and greet with the dog, they quickly determined she was far too energetic and playful for them. They needed a dog that was mellow and easygoing.

Rather than give up, they continued to look at the available dogs, many of which were barking and jumping in their kennels excitedly. Eventually, they walked past Dreamy's kennel. Their eyes locked on Dreamy as she remained slouched up against the siding, not making a peep.

They were transfixed by her sweet eyes and calm demeanor, so Natalie and Ian requested to see her outside the kennel. The second she was brought out into the play yard, Dreamy's gentle personality began to reveal itself. She had a raw sweetness to her, perhaps enhanced by her years mothering puppies.

At one point, Ian sat down on a bench and Dreamy hopped up next to him before placing her paw on his lap. It was a picturesque moment that sealed the deal for them wanting to adopt her. Five weeks after being picked up on the side of the road, Dreamy had found her forever family!

During the first few months with Natalie and Ian, Dreamy was a little skeptical of her new beginning. Her tail remained between her legs, and it was as if she felt unsure whether this was just a long field trip. Over time, she realized it was no temporary arrangement, but rather a permanent home with people she could trust. As she grew more and more relaxed, she started warming up. After a while, it became clear she was an old soul with a big heart.

Now fully confident in her new home, Dreamy is absolutely enamored with Natalie and Ian. She often places her paws on them if they stop petting her, just like she did at the shelter during their initial meeting. She never wants to be left behind, so Natalie and Ian make every attempt to bring her with them whenever possible. They consider her their road dog.

Dreamy has accompanied them on many island adventures and all in all, she has lived the ultimate Hawaiian dream during her new chapter. Whether it is hiking through mes-merizing nature trails or splashing in the gorgeous island waves, she relishes the stunning

Hawaiian sceneries. In fact, her retirement adventures would make almost any human envious.

When they go on family walks, Dreamy always calls the shots. When she decides she is done walking, she will sit down abruptly. While her facial expressions are often as unchanging as a champion poker player, she does get moments of puppy-like excitement. She has also started to enjoy playing, despite it originally seeming like a foreign concept to her. Natalie has even taught Dreamy how to play fetch, thereby breaking the misconception that "you can't teach an old dog new tricks." As it turns out, playing fetch is actually one of her favorite activities now.

Since welcoming Dreamy into their lives, Natalie and Ian officially consider themselves dog people. While they had never really considered adopting an older dog, their experiences with Dreamy have shown them the loyalty and love senior dogs can offer. Now, they are passionate supporters of rescuing senior dogs.

As for Dreamy, well, she plans to keep living the dream one adventure at a time with her parents by her side.

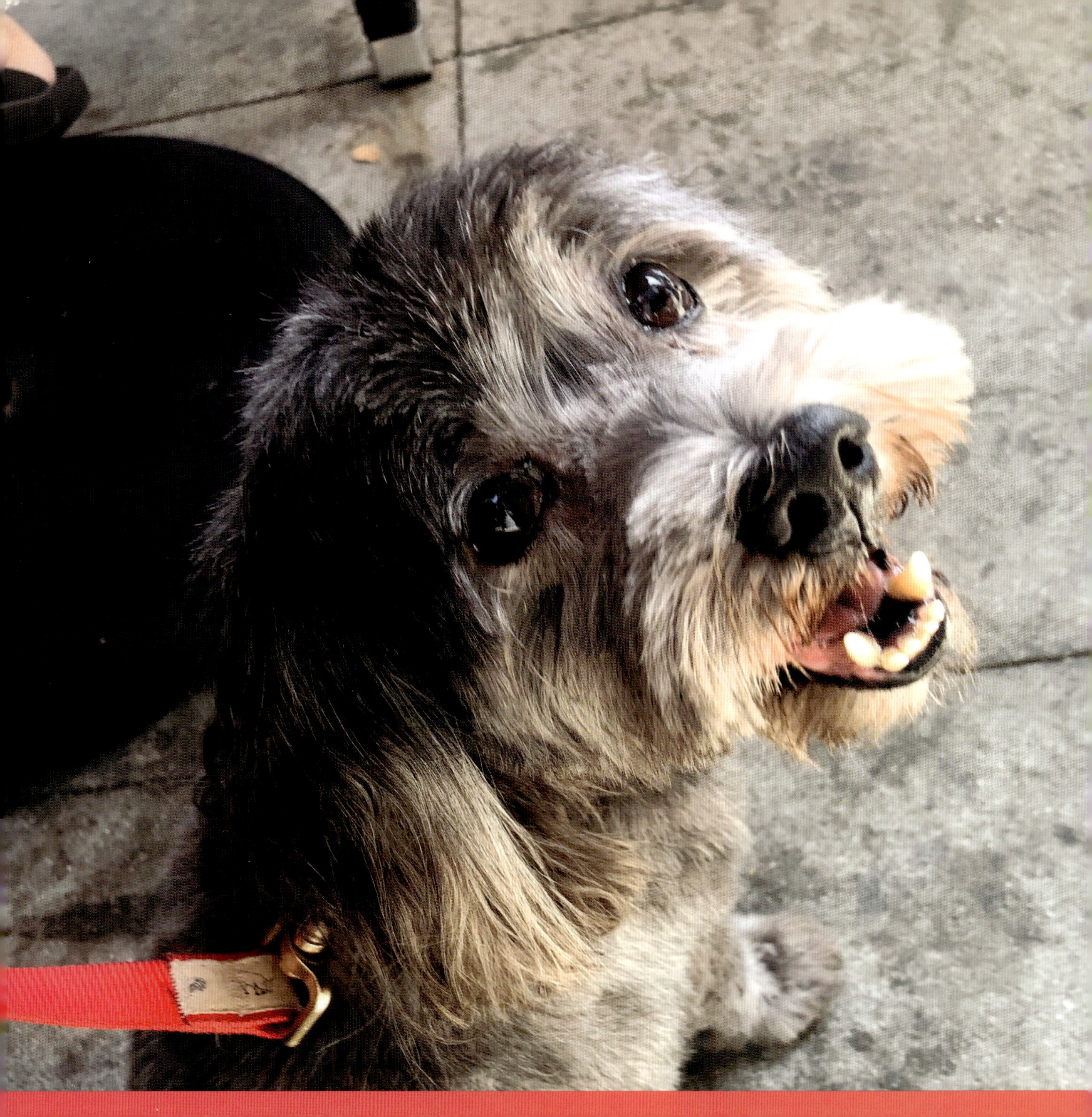

BOOM, 11

Before becoming a senior rescue, Boom endured some pretty severe hardships. His former owner was an elderly woman who struggled to properly take care of Boom, as well as her other dog and cat. Sadly, she passed away inside her home, and her three pets were forced to fend for themselves for several days before anyone found them. Once discovered, Boom and his pet siblings were taken in by local rescues. While his younger doggy brother was quickly adopted, Boom was left waiting for his forever home.

Kathryn of California was looking to adopt a dog. Because she lived in a Los Angeles apartment, she recognized her living situation would be best suited for an elderly dog. She first took notice of Boom after seeing his photo posted on the PetFinder website. Although his outward appearance was disheveled and unkempt, Kathryn undeniably felt it was love at first sight.

She wanted to adopt him immediately, but had some trouble pinpointing his exact location. Determined to find him, she began attending pop-up adoption events at local pet stores and shelters. After a couple weeks of unsuccessful search efforts, she learned Boom was being cared for by the Amanda Foundation.

Kathryn's persistence continued as she called multiple times per day to arrange a time to come see Boom. The stars finally aligned, and Kathryn was able to meet Boom face to face soon thereafter. While she envisioned their first meeting would be filled with kisses and snuggles, this was sadly not how the event actually unfolded. Boom's past had made a significant impact on his personality and behavior, so he was very timid and confused during their first interaction.

Fortunately, his standoffishness did not hinder Kathryn's strong desire to adopt him. He was dirty and rough around the edges, but in Kathryn's eyes, he was the perfect dog. She considers their initial meeting to be one of the best days of her life.

Boom took some time to adjust to his new life, and he was quite nervous at first. Normalcies—such as sleeping in a bed—were foreign and mystifying to him. Kathryn initially worried something was terribly wrong because Boom's tail remained tucked between his legs at all times.

To help him transition, Kathryn offered him love and patience. As Boom slowly began feeling comfortable in his new environment, his tail started to rise, and his true personality emerged. It turns out that beneath all that grime and dirt is a loving old dog who is both affectionate and sassy.

Now an avid snuggler, Boom proudly and willingly uses doggy stairs to climb atop the bed whenever he wants a snuggle session. He wakes Kathryn every morning by adorably placing his head under her hand. He will also fall fast asleep anytime he is in her arms for more than a few minutes.

Kathryn has learned that Boom is surprisingly a punctual dog, despite having little to no structure in his former home. Now, every day when the clock hits five o'clock, Boom knows it is dinner time. To make sure Kathryn cannot forget this, he will cheekily lie down with his back paws spread apart and repeatedly emit a pigeon-like noise until his dinner is ready.

Even when it is not dinner time, coaxing food out of people remains a common trend for Boom. When he wants a treat, he will showcase his most convincing puppy dog eyes or gain attention by any means necessary.

Boom has a lot of roar left in his engine, despite his relatively old age. He enjoys accompanying Kathryn for long walks on the beach. In fact, he enjoys this so much that he wildly spins in circles any time he sees her reaching for his harness.

While Boom gets very excited for walks, he becomes the most excited when Kathryn returns home, even if her departure only lasted an hour. In fact, he becomes so overcome with emotion that he will hug her leg. Although this is a frequent occurrence, it never ceases to melt Kathryn's heart. She appreciates all of Boom's quirks and adores witnessing his personality unfold.

All the goofiness and lovable sass aside, Boom is truly at peace living his new chapter with Kathryn. His tail was anchored between his legs at the beginning, but now it refuses to stop wagging!

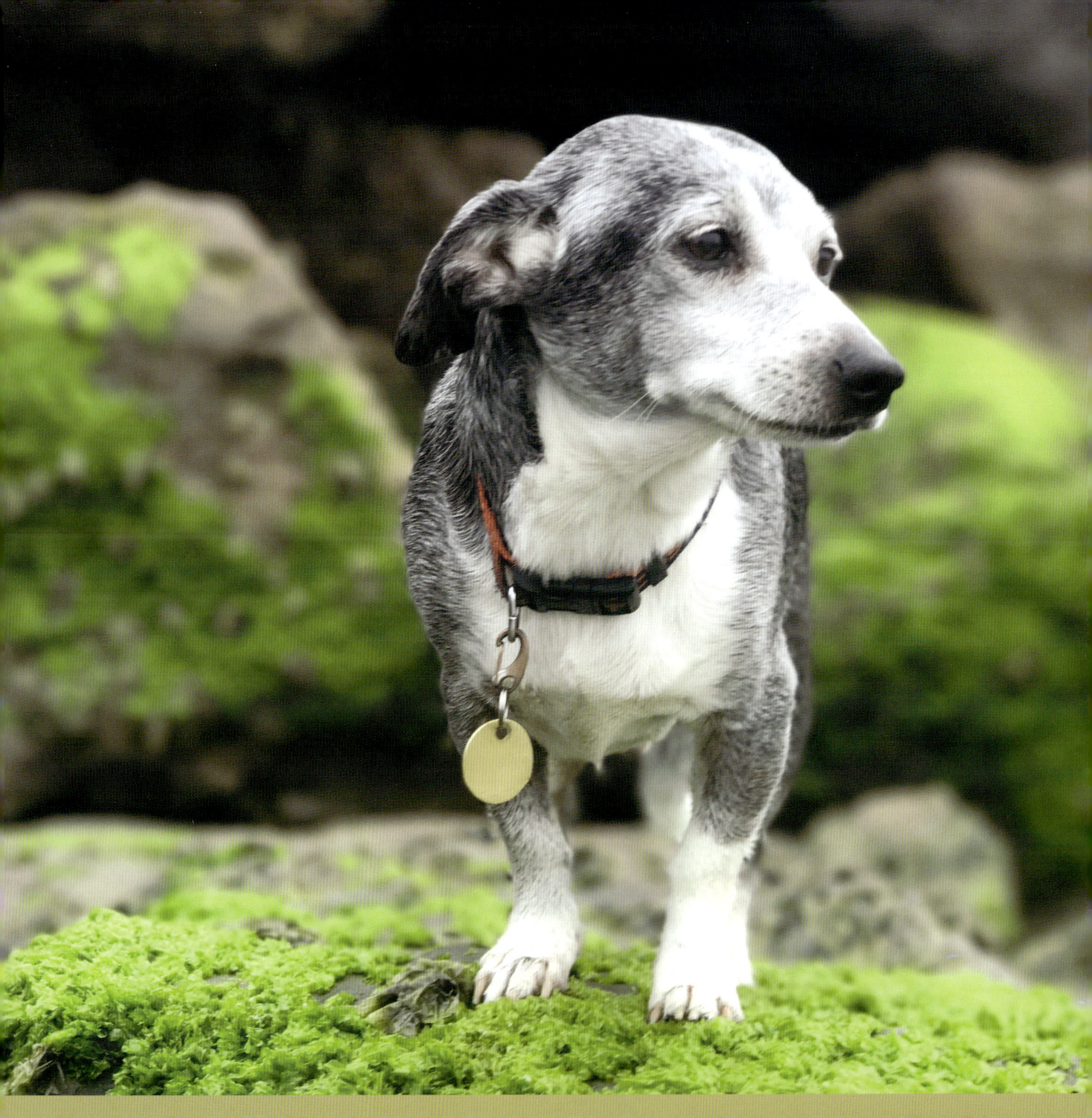

ROADIE, 13

During her frequent commutes to work, Elizabeth had come across many unattended dogs roaming the streets of downtown Los Angeles. A compassionate animal supporter, she always found a way to cajole them into her car and safely drop them off at the North Central Animal Shelter on Lacy Street.

One day, she spotted a miniature, black and white-coated dog weaving in and out of traffic on one of the city's busiest four-way streets. After witnessing the old dog narrowly avoid getting hit multiple times, she bravely parked her car horizontally to block oncoming traffic. To her surprise, the frightened old dog was quick to stop for her as his tail wagged timidly between his legs.

As Elizabeth scooped him up, she noticed he was covered in fleas and had chewed his back hips to the point that open wounds had formed. Rightfully concerned, she took him directly to a vet and felt a momentary sense of relief when the vet discovered the elderly dog had a microchip. Unfortunately, no one answered when they called the phone number associated with the microchip.

In the meantime, Elizabeth paid for him to receive proper medication for his fleas and undergo a much-needed nail cutting. After deciding he needed a name, at least temporarily until his owner could be reached, she started to call him "Roadie," a fitting tribute to the location of their initial meeting.

While she continued to wait for the owner to return her call, Elizabeth took Roadie to a co-worker's house for a bath and some rest. She was stunned by how quickly he became attached to her. He followed her from room to room throughout the day. As the day's end approached, Roadie's former owner had still not returned the many calls Elizabeth left him/her. Worried about dropping him off at the shelter, especially because of his age and condition, Elizabeth opted to take him back to her apartment, even though her apartment complex did not allow pets.

When they arrived at her apartment, Roadie's former owner finally called back. The woman explained she had fell on hard times and could no longer care for Snoopy, which was the name originally given to him. Rather than respond with angst, Elizabeth offered to care for him. While she certainly wished the owner had surrendered Roadie in a more humane and appropriate way, Elizabeth considered the opportunity to adopt such a wonderful dog to be a hidden blessing.

After she hung up the phone that day, both her and Roadie's lives were instantly changed for the better. After realizing he steadfastly did not respond to "Snoopy," Elizabeth decided to keep the name she had given him earlier that day: Roadie.

Roadie instantly took a liking to his new life chapter; however, it was quickly discovered that he has pretty intense separation anxiety, which is not surprising given his past abandonment. Instead of leaving him alone to be at the mercy of his anxiety, Elizabeth and her boyfriend, Walter, now take Roadie just about everywhere with them, even to outings such as the movie theater. As long as he is by their sides, Roadie is calm and relaxed. In fact, every person who meets him describes him as, "the chill-est creature they have ever met."

While he is believed to be around thirteen years old, he still gets sudden, intense bursts of puppy energy about once a day. During these sporadic energy gusts, Roadie exhibits a look of pure joy which has an infectiously positive effect on anyone lucky enough to witness it.

All his puppy-like episodes aside, Roadie is still an old dog who loves his sleep. He has especially taken a liking to jumping into bed, nosing his way under the covers, and then falling fast asleep.

One of Roadie's favorite activities is to ride in the car with his head hanging outside the window. While the wind hits his graying muzzle, he expresses an overall feeling of satisfaction and serenity as he gazes at the outside world.

Because Elizabeth and Walter's apartment complexes both did not allow pets, they were inspired to expedite their plans to purchase their first home together. They now live in a house with a massive backyard that was specifically chosen with Roadie in mind. He loves to take advantage of his new space by running freely through the grass in a Bambi-like stride.

Elizabeth and Walter's whole lives have changed immensely, and for the better, ever since Roadie entered the picture. They credit him with being the force that helped them reach the happy place they are at now. Fittingly, they often refer to Roadie as their little gift from the universe.

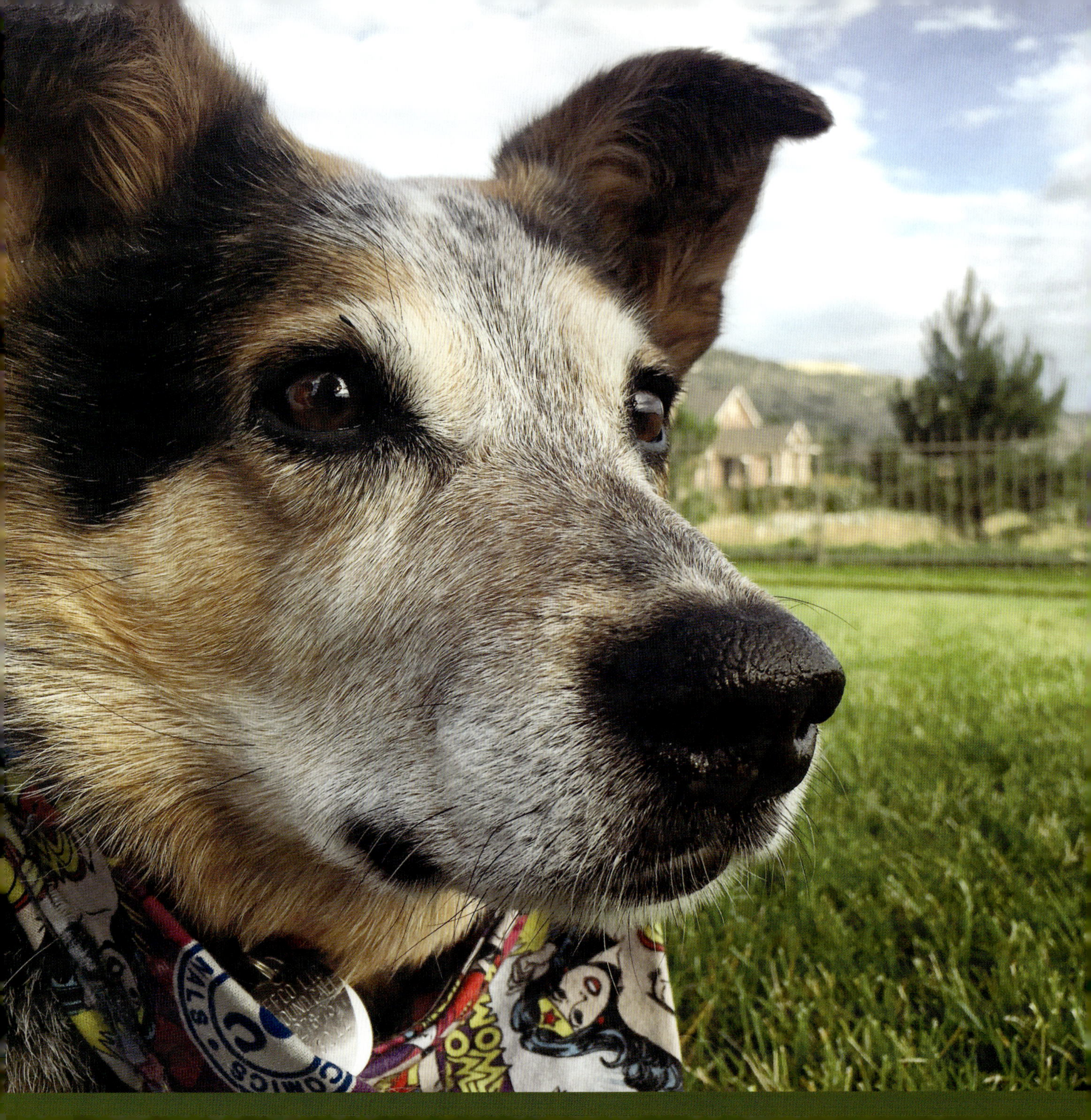
WOW

TICK, 10

Very few details are known about Tick's life before she was picked up as a stray senior and taken in by the Humane Society of Fremont County (HSFC). At the time, she was overweight and suffering from severe arthritis pain.

She was soon sent to another rescue organization in closer proximity to a metropolitan area in hopes of increasing her exposure to possible adopters. Sadly, the new organization labeled her as aggressive and quickly returned her to HSFC for possible euthanasia. Fortunately, HSFC did not concur with this new characterization, so they began searching for a hospice-type arrangement for Tick.

Brittany, a longtime supporter of cattle dog rescue groups, stepped up to serve as Tick's foster mom. At the time, Tick was going by a different name: Julia Roberts. Brittany decided Tick needed her own, unique name to honor her new beginning. From that moment on, she has been known as Tick!

After discovering Tick had a whole lot of fight left in her, Brittany began to heavily network her through rescue organizations' social media channels. She posted on a cattle dog group with over 10,000 members. The post received a lot of attention, but ultimately did not lead to Tick securing a home. Brittany aimed to reach a broader network, so she contacted Susie's Senior Dogs.

Britt (not to be confused with foster mom, Brittany) and Connor had long followed Susie's Senior Dogs on social media. They had not yet come across a posting for an adoptable senior in the Denver area, so they were ecstatic when Tick's post popped up on their feeds. They were touched by Tick's story and fell hard for her wholesome eyes and floppy ears.

Rather than rushing to fill out the application prematurely, the couple carefully considered whether the timing was right for them to proceed. When Tick's posting was redisplayed two days later after no adoption leads, the couple decided it was kismet. They reached out to Brittany, completed the adoption application, and waited anxiously while a photograph of Tick hung on their bulletin board.

A few days later, they received the call they had been waiting for; their adoption application had been accepted and the only box left to check was a home visit. Soon thereafter, Tick arrived for her home visit, and she has been a part of their lives ever since. Tick initially did not engage in cuddling, but over time she has become more like Velcro to her new parents. She frequently likes to bombard them with kisses on the face.

While she certainly has a sassy side and even a Chewbacca roar to match, Tick has a mature and nurturing presence. She is known for being the neighborhood greeter, always stopping to meet each new human. Her affection for Britt and Connor runs deep, and she can instantly sense when they are stressed or hurting.

She is an innate creature of habit and makes sure her parents stay true to their routine. When it is time for dinner, she will lead them to the kitchen to start cooking. Britt and

Connor are good about maintaining Tick's schedule, and they ensure her days always end with a nice tooth brushing.

A true cattle dog, Tick's greatest interest is spending time outdoors. It does not matter if she is paw-deep in a snow pile or if her coat is glistening in the summer sun, Tick is quite content with any weather condition Mother Nature delivers.

After her arthritis medications were adjusted appropriately, Tick began to build up an incredible amount of muscle for an older dog. She now proudly walks several miles each day through the stunning Colorado scenery. She is known for sporting colorful bandanas from her sizable, eclectic collection of over twenty bandanas!

Tick is also a big fan of being a passenger on car rides. Britt and Connor are always transparent with Tick about where their car rides are headed, and they never try to trick her into going to the vet...although admittedly, she does not seem to mind the vet too much. Her favorite destination is always Grandma's house. There, she likes to explore the yard and spacious kitchen, but her favorite part is connecting and showing affection to more people she loves.

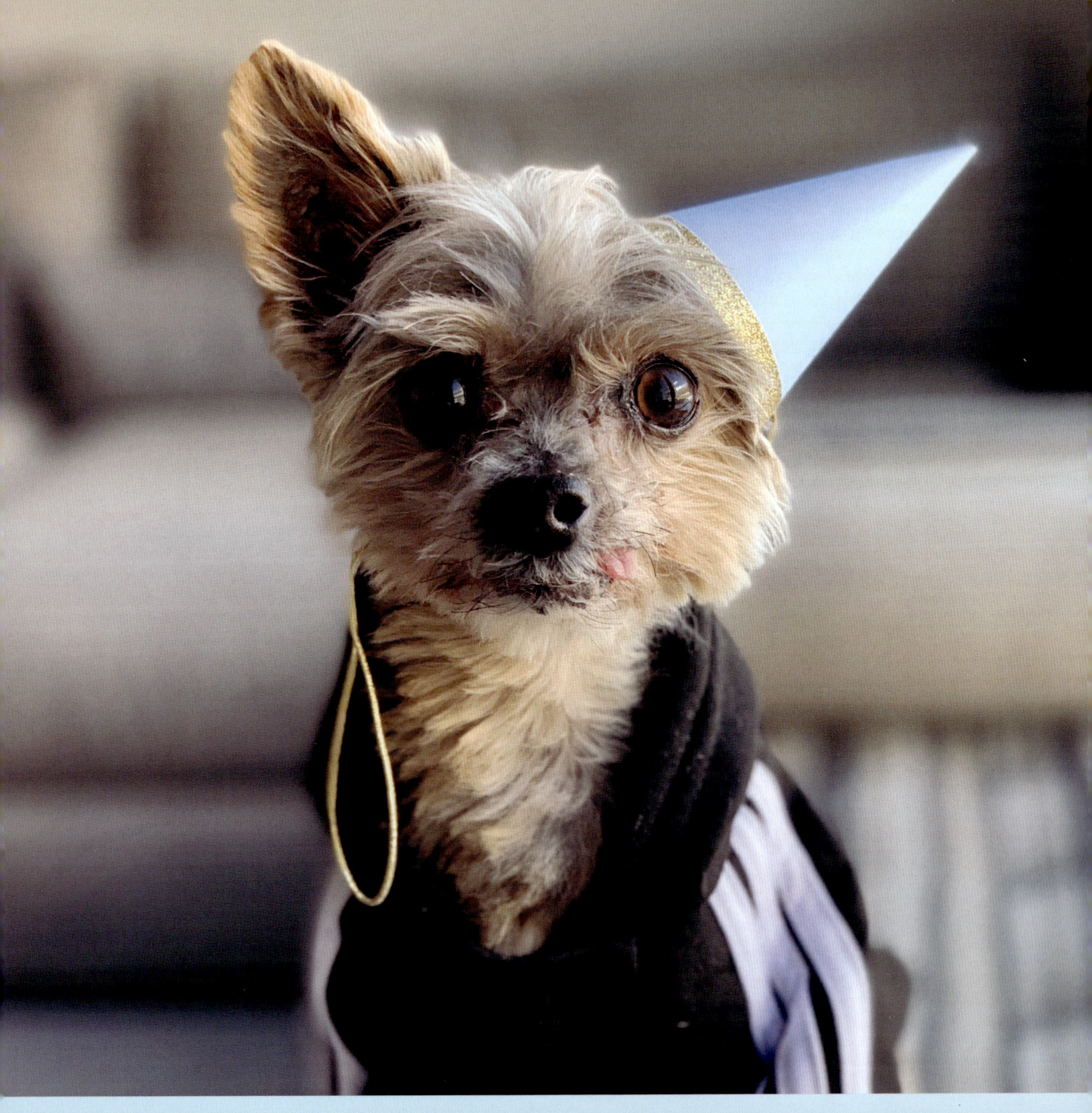

GUS, 12

For most of Gus' life, he suffered through the harsh realities of living in a puppy mill. He was badly neglected while being continuously used for breeding. When he was twelve years old and considered too old to serve as an asset for the breeding business, he was abandoned outside a veterinary office in Salt Lake City, Utah.

When the veterinary office discovered him, they were faced with a difficult decision as to how to proceed. Because Gus was quite elderly, in bad shape, and without a home, they considered possible euthanasia. As little Gus was on the examination table and the shot was about to be delivered to end his life, a kindhearted, young vet tech named Emily intervened to halt the procedure because she recognized that Gus had a lot of life left to experience!

For two weeks, Emily kept him at the veterinary office and provided him with the medical care he had never previously received. She would selflessly stay after hours to run blood tests, pull out his teeth, perform X-rays, and groom him. She soon realized that Gus was a relatively healthy older dog who just needed to be loved.

The entire veterinary office began rallying behind Gus. Realizing he had a second chance at life, they created a bucket list for Gus that they hoped he could one day complete if the right person came around. The bucket list included featured items such as watching the sunset, visiting a dog park, and having a portrait created of him. He soon earned the loving nickname of the "Bucket List Dog."

Another woman, by complete chance and fate, happened to meet Gus when she brought her pet to the veterinary office. Her heart broke as she learned of Gus' story and how he was searching for his forever home. The woman immediately called her niece, Calin, whom she believed might be a good match for Gus. Sure enough, Calin was also touched by Gus' story, so much so that she came to pick him up that night.

When Gus first arrived at her home, Calin believed he was deaf because he did not respond in any way to noises or attempts at interaction. Because he was completely silent, she also wondered whether his voice box had been removed or damaged. It turns out that Gus' silence and lack of engagement were not signs of medical issues, but rather just a coping mechanism he had developed after many years of fearfully living in the puppy mill.

Calin did not give up hope on her new underdog companion, and she was willing to ease him into feeling comfortable with human interaction. Over time, he slowly learned to trust humans and to understand noises. Now, he loves to hear his name being called. Humorously, he likes to smack his lips as a way to communicate with her. He has also started letting out an occasional bark. Because he only weighs a mere four pounds, each of Gus' barks impresses not only himself, but also anyone who happens to hear them.

Due to a lack of dental care in his earlier life, Gus now has no teeth and his tongue dangles from the side of his mouth. His unique smile only adds to his charisma. A naturally photogenic dog with a puppy-like look, he is always willing to dress up in doggy costumes and pose for a photo op.

Gus is still sporadically energetic, even in his old age. He loves running around and smelling every single tree at the park. He also likes to sprint from the elevator back to Calin's apartment every night. When he eventually gets tired, he likes to bury his tiny body in the arms of Calin and her boyfriend, Tanner.

As Gus has soaked in the securities of his new chapter, he has successfully crossed off a few items on his bucket list, like having a birthday party thrown on his "gotcha" day. Throughout his new journey, Calin has maintained a great friendship with Emily and provides her with updates on Gus' progress and adventures. She often visits the veterinary office and makes sure to bring Gus along to see his old friends.

Through Calin and Tanner's love and support, Gus has finally learned what a home really is. His story is a superb reminder that every dog deserves a second chance at life.

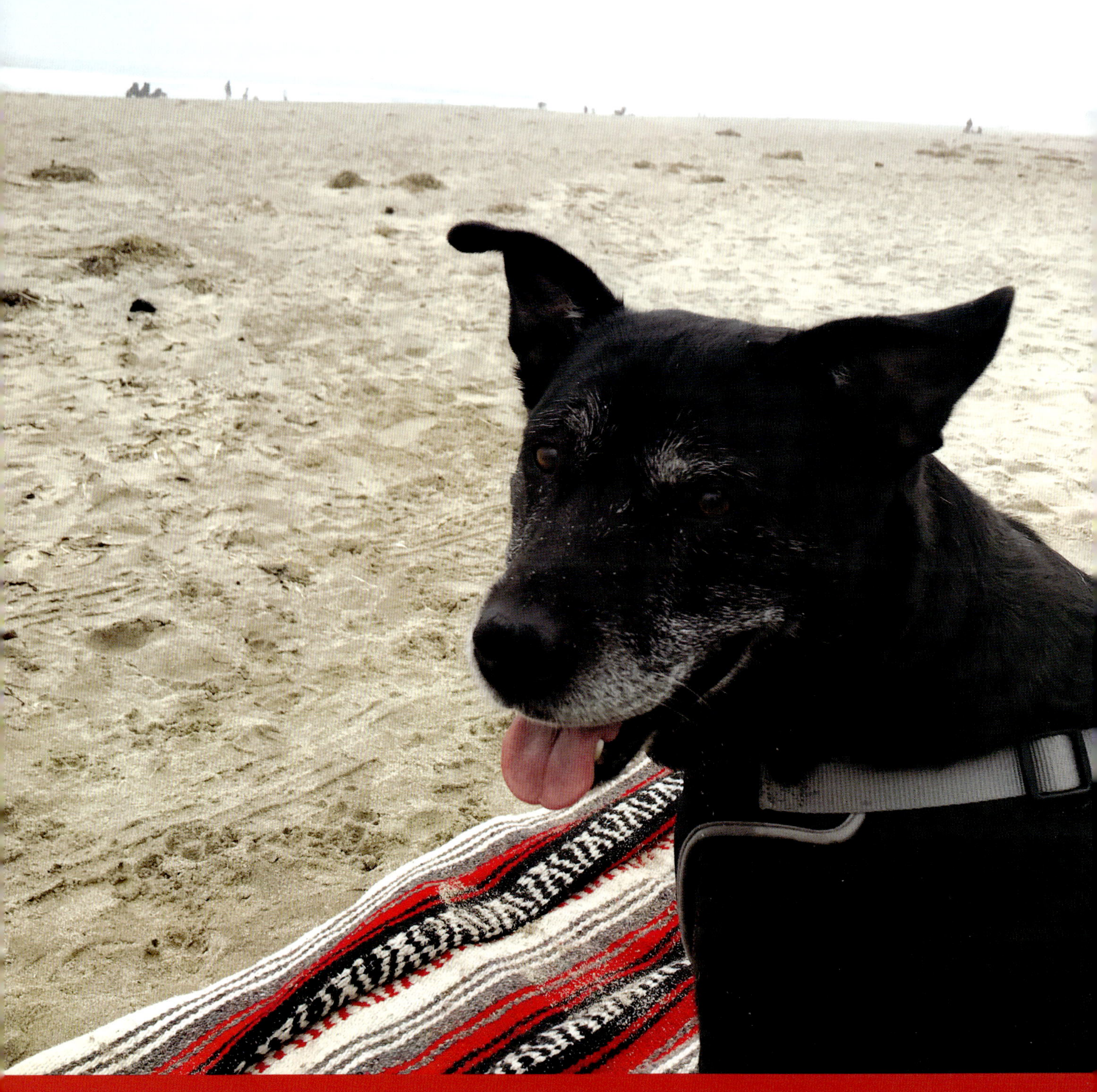

DIOGI, 10

At eight weeks old, Diogi (appropriately pronounced "D-O-G") was adopted by a family from the Multnomah County Animal Shelter. An endearing puppy, it was no surprise she was chosen quickly. She then spent the next eight years living with her family before they decided to move and ultimately surrender her to the Oregon Humane Society.

By this point, Diogi had developed small tumors all over her body, so the shelter arranged for her to undergo surgery to address the tumors. Fortunately, the surgery was a success and there were no signs of cancer. Diogi recovered at the shelter while she waited for a new, forever family to come find her.

Newlyweds Jenn and Kevin of Oregon had a pure love for older dogs, and they knew they could provide a loving and happy environment for a senior dog. For over a month, they had been visiting the shelter in search of an older rescue dog to bring home with them. During those initial shelter drop-ins, they met a few senior dogs, but each time, something did not feel quite right.

One weekend, Jenn and Kevin decided to take another walk through the Oregon Humane Society. They soon laid eyes on Diogi, who was wearing a "cone of dignity" from her recent surgery. Her body was turned away from the front gate, tightly curled in a ball. They called her name eagerly, beckoning her to move toward the door so they could get a better look at her, but she did not budge. While there was no magical eye-locking moment, something about her made the couple curious, and they did not want to give up on her just yet.

They arranged for a meet and greet in the designated playroom. While they waited, they were informed that Diogi was timid and afraid of people, especially men. Given that Kevin stands six feet, six inches tall and rocks a hearty beard, they determined he would be the ultimate test to whether she was actually fearful of men.

Despite the initial uncertainties, Diogi lit up the room immediately after entering and chased a ball gleefully. Jenn and Kevin sat on the floor with her, and she took a liking to them both in a heartbeat. She even rolled over willingly and let them scratch her belly. As their hearts melted, the couple knew they had to have her. She went home with them that day!

From the moment she first hopped in their car, Diogi has not stopped smiling. She transitioned into her new home seamlessly, and if you did not know any better, you might think that she has been living with Jenn and Kevin all her life.

The couple quickly discovered that Diogi is quite the goofy companion. In spite of her greying beard and arthritic knees, she has been known to scale the kitchen counter with the agility of an Olympic hurdler. A very food-motivated dog, Diogi also has a bit of a mischievous side. Shortly after arriving in her new home, a pot roast was left out on the counter to thaw while Jenn and Kevin ran some errands. When they arrived home, they found butcher paper strewn all over the living room while Diogo lay on the couch, casually gnawing into a partially defrosted roast. Admittedly, they were quite amazed by her dexterity, but have since opted to leave open food atop the refrigerator.

Diogi has large, bat-like ears, which provide insights as to what she is thinking depending on the directions they are pointing. In fact, she has the clever skill of being able to turn one ear forward to listen to her humans, while her other ear leans back so she can hear the background noises of chattering birds and squirrels in the trees.

Like many dogs, Diogi is a big fan of riding in the car. If she sees her parents moving toward the car, she persistently searches for any possible way to accompany them. When they let her come along, her sweet spot is in the backseat, resting her chin on the window frame, eyes closed, with the wind in her ears.

One of her favorite activities is to go camping with her parents. She loves the new smells, the people, soaking in the outdoor air, and snuggling in her very own sleeping bag. She also enjoys the nature walks, and when her arthritis kicks in on longer walks, she gets to be pulled in a wagon.

While Diogi relishes all the adventures of her new chapter, her favorite place to be is curled up in between her parents on the couch with one of her many stuffed animals.

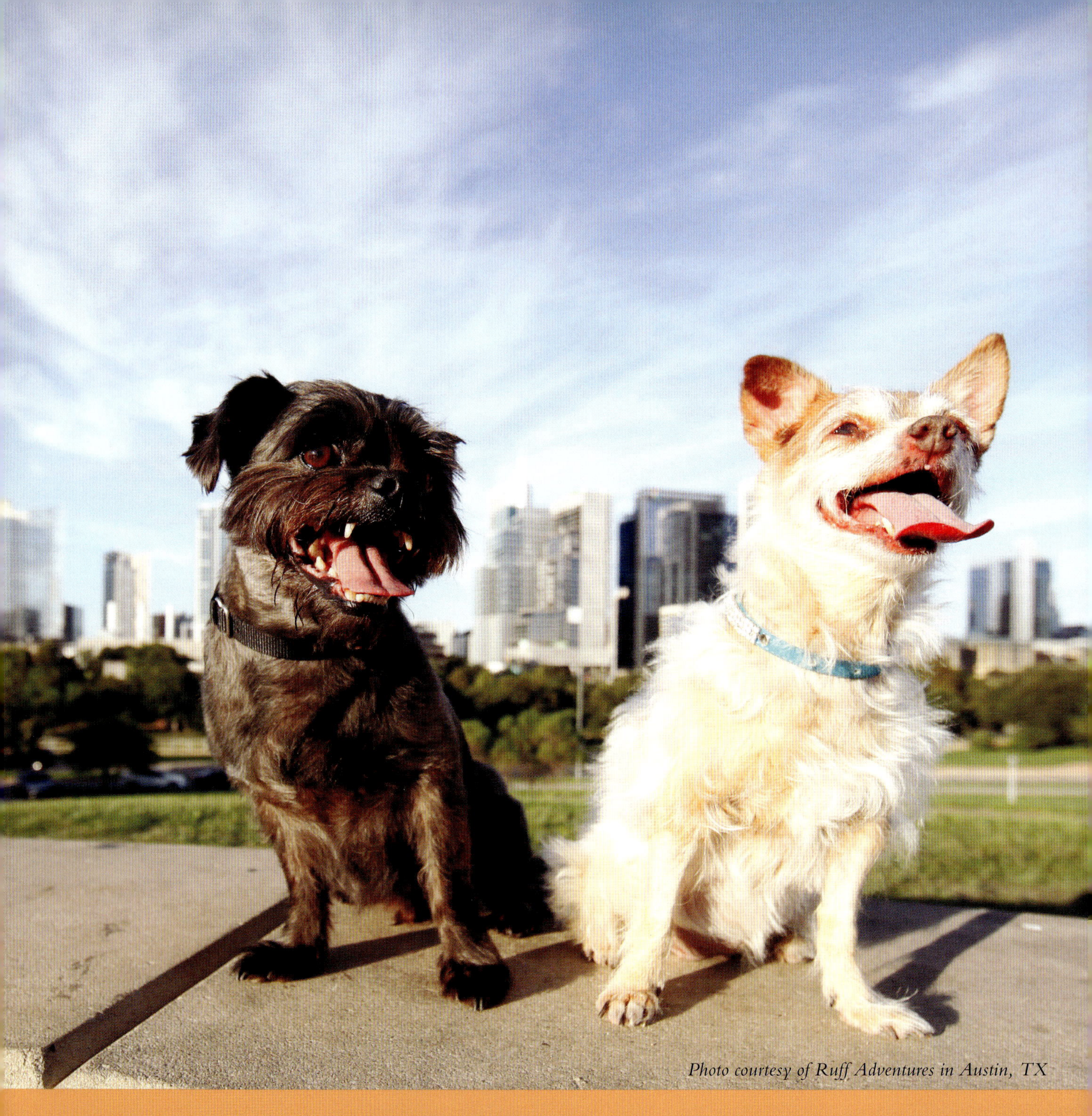
Photo courtesy of Ruff Adventures in Austin, TX

HARLEY, 11; AND PHYLLIS, 14

After losing their dog Eddie, Nicole and Bryce of Texas noticed their remaining senior dog, Grace, was showing signs of loneliness. They had just begun to consider adopting another dog when a little scruffy, old dog with an endearing underbite appeared on their television screen.

This senior dog—named Sunny Boy, at the time—was being featured as the local news station's adoptable pet of the week. The segment indicated he was an adoptable senior, and it was assumed from his broken leg and pelvis that he had been hit by a car.

Immediately, Nicole and Bryce strongly believed his age and demeanor would make him the perfect companion for Grace. They knew they had to have him, so they made sure to be the first in line at the mobile adoption event he was appearing at. After a successful first interaction between Sunny Boy and Grace, they filled out the necessary paperwork and brought him home.

Nicole and Bryce quickly realized that Sunny Boy did not respond to his given name. They decided his new beginning should come with a suitable dog name, and he was henceforth known as Harley! During their first few weeks together, Harley was often found timidly hiding under Nicole and Bryce's bed. This was surprising because, in their household, dog beds are scattered everywhere, and pets are always permitted on the furniture.

Nicole and Bryce understood that his initial behavior was just a by-product of his past and that he would need to learn to trust humans again. They were patient as they slowly earned Harley's trust. It ended up taking almost a year for his initial apprehensions to completely subside and for his confidence to regrow.

A stark contrast to his early days of hiding, Harley is now a cheerful ball of love and affection. He has even become the family's comedian. About once a week, he goes into full-blown "zoomies," which consists of his eyes growing wide as he accelerates in the fastest circles. He is sometimes referred to as a snapping turtle because if a fly, dust, or shadow floats near his face, he bites at it. He almost always misses, but his attempts are quite a sight to behold. He also has a series of goofy facial expressions, which evoke smiles in almost every person he encounters.

Along Harley's road to emotional recovery, he and Grace formed an incredible bond. When Grace passed away a year after his arrival, the entire family was devastated. Nicole and Bryce could tell Harley missed the companionship of another dog, so they again considered adopting a senior rescue.

Nicole soon came across a posting from Austin Pets Alive! about an adoptable senior dog named Diamond who was being held at the Austin Animal Center. The post indicated she was exceptionally sweet but had been constantly overlooked due to her age. Nicole and Bryce were immediately drawn to foster, so they went to meet her and brought Harley along.

When they arrived, the shelter staff explained that Diamond had lived with a loving owner for many years. When her owner went to jail, Diamond was passed around among family members and friends until her eventual surrender.

After meeting Diamond and hearing more details of her story, Nicole and Bryce happily took her in as a foster. Two weeks later, they decided to officially adopt her, and they soon changed her name to Phyllis after Phyllis Diller, specifically because she also had wild blonde hair that stuck out in every which way.

While her transformation was not as drastic as Harley's, Phyllis has become more social in her new environment. She loves to greet visitors and enjoys snuggling, especially with Bryce. Phyllis loves going on neighborhood walks. Interestingly, her preferred walking path is on the curb, likely because it is an ideal width for her tiny feet. Despite her age, she balances and maneuvers on the curb quite well.

Phyllis' most endearing behavior occurs just before meals when she sprints wildly around the house. Her daily dashes are so amusing because they seem so contradictory to her fragile, older body. Once her food is served, she takes a few minutes to eat it, then she goes right back to bed as if nothing ever happened.

All in all, Nicole and Bryce have grown more passionate about rescuing senior dogs after their experiences with Harley and Phyllis. They plan to continue adopting the elderly, often overlooked dogs in the future. In their eyes, senior dog adoption offers an incredible opportunity to provide a great life to a dog who needs it, and it also provides these deserving dogs with an environment to heal and grow.

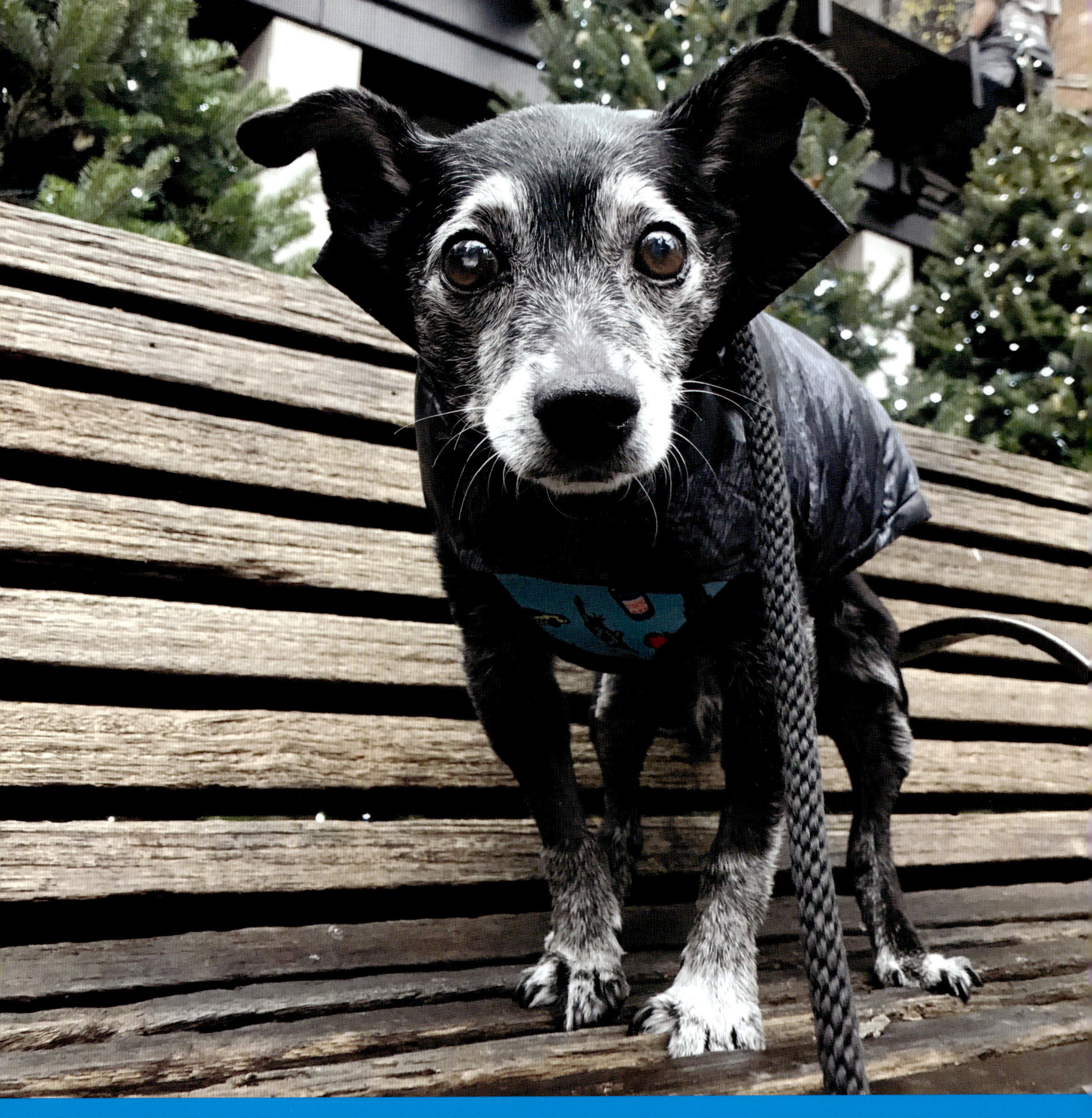

ELMER, 14

Roughly two months after Hurricane Sandy pulverized the East Coast, a group of teenagers discovered a little black dog wandering the streets of Queens, New York. The sympathetic teenagers gently scooped up the dog and placed him in the safe hands of an animal rescue organization known as Bobbi and the Strays. The dog, who was then given the name Elmer, was estimated to be around eight years old. When he arrived in the shelter's care, he had a large growth on his back, so they soon arranged for him to undergo a surgery to have it removed.

Josephine and Chris of Manhattan, New York made a stop into the shelter with hopes of finding a new furry companion that was suited for their lifestyle. They were particularly interested in adopting a senior because they recognized older dogs are typically calmer and more likely to have already been trained. In their eyes, it did not matter how many years they could spend with their future dog because they were certain every moment spent together would be precious.

Elmer was still recovering from his surgery when Josephine and Chris first met him that day. He donned a cone around his neck, and he had five inches of stitches running down his lower back. Despite being in recovery, Elmer lit up when he saw Josephine and Chris. He was bursting with happiness as his bottom wiggled uncontrollably. The couple considered his excitement to be infectious, and they knew he was the dog for them.

They quickly put in an application to adopt him, and they were approved adopters after a successful home visit.

It took about one year of being in his new home for Elmer to realize Josephine and Chris were not going anywhere. At first, he was a bit grumpy toward people and dogs, and he would exhibit nervousness at the veterinarian's office and when visiting a groomer. Elmer has since mellowed out and become accustomed to his new, spoiled life that is filled with many adventures and constant affection.

Elmer loves being outside, and he relishes sniffing every smell that New York City has to offer. His devoted parents take him on at least five walks a day, and they always ensure he is dressed appropriately for the weather. During the harsh New York City winters, he stays warm by wearing many fashionable layers, including puffy jackets, scarves, and sweaters. In the hot summer months, he showcases his vast array of colorful harnesses.

Not surprisingly, Elmer frequently receives a lot of attention during his walks. He savors this attention and has even started expecting people to stop for him. He also likes to casually sniff the legs of passers-by because he firmly believes he knows everyone.

Since he lives in one of the world's most famous tourist destinations, it is only fitting that Elmer loves sightseeing. He visits Rockefeller Center a few times a year, including his annual visit to its iconic Christmas tree. He also likes to go to Central Park during off-leash hours because it presents an opportunity to meet other city dogs. While visiting Central Park, Josephine and Chris always make sure he gets a photo in front of the famous Bethesda Fountain. Since Elmer travels well, he is included in family holidays. He has become a "grandchild" and "nephew," and he and his cousin, Wiley, look forward to special treats at family gatherings.

An exploratory dog, Elmer loves to partake in "find the treat" games. Typically, the treats are hidden in advance under cups, in a puzzle toy, or in a multi-part plush toy. No matter where his parents decide to conceal the treats, Elmer always finds them in the end.

Over time, Elmer has become more affectionate, but he is also still adamantly independent. He only likes to accept hugs and kisses on his own terms. Fortunately, his terms have loosened and allowed for more frequent affection as the years have passed. He is also a passionate greeter. Regardless of whether his parents are gone for five minutes or five hours, Elmer greets them with the same "wiggle butt" excitement he exhibited the day they first met. His greetings always serve as a source of pure joy for them.

It has been more than six years since Josephine and Chris welcomed Elmer into their lives. As they initially anticipated, they have cherished every single moment they have spent with Elmer.

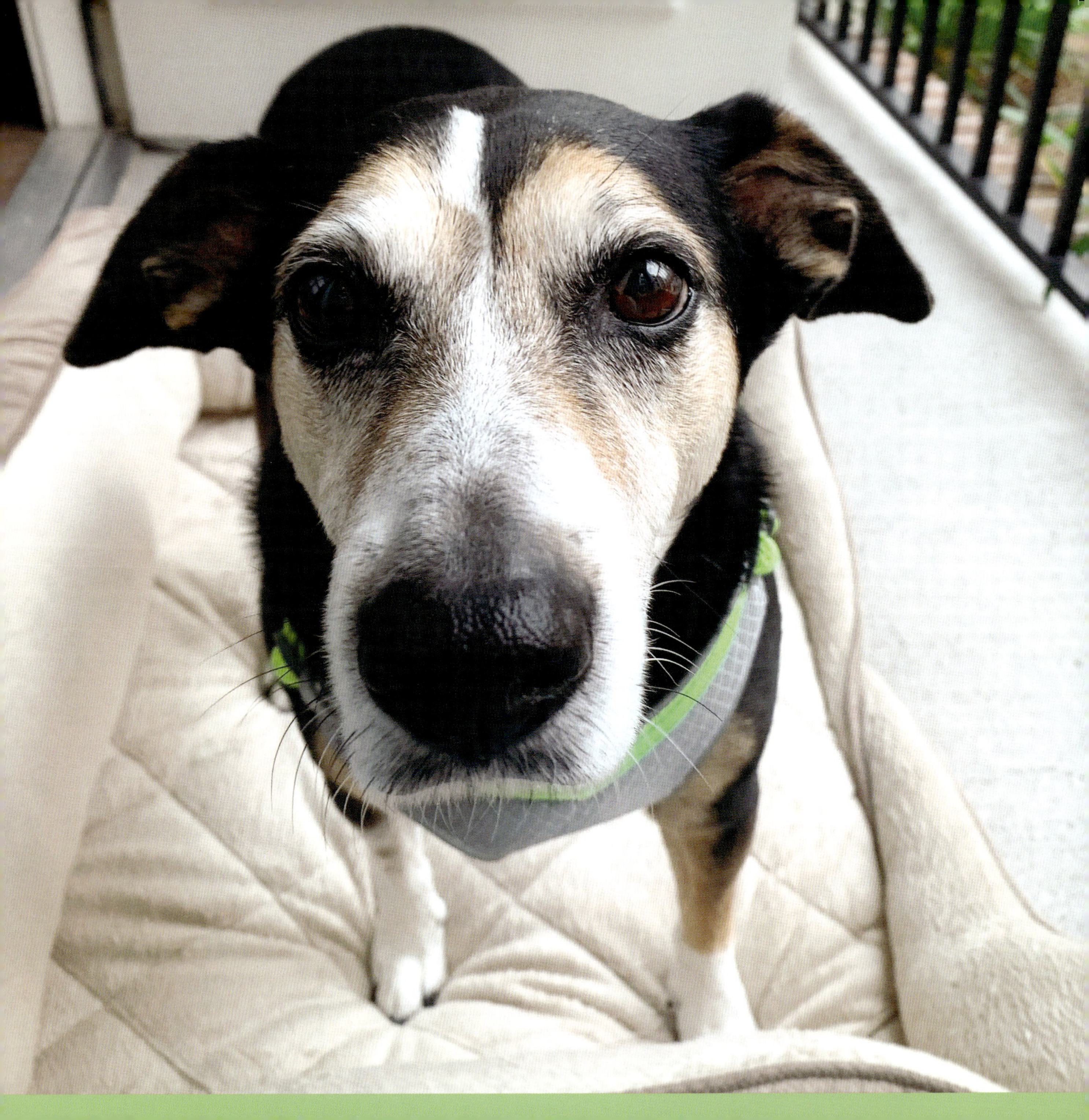

PRISCILLA, 12

Priscilla's road to finding her forever home was a long one, but fortunately, she received quite a bit of support along the way. Her story began when she and her brother, who at the time were just puppies, were found running down the side of a rural South Carolina road. After being picked up by a good Samaritan, they were taken in by the compassionate people at the Hallie Hill Animal Sanctuary in Hollywood, South Carolina.

They were soon given the names Elvis and Priscilla. Together, the two were more than just siblings, but rather a dynamic duo. Because of their incredible bond, they were always kept together at the Hallie Hill Animal Sanctuary and were only available as a paired adoption, in order to keep them from being separated. While they were never successfully adopted together, the pair lived in harmony for more than eleven years under excellent care at the sanctuary.

Sadly, everything changed for Priscilla when Elvis passed away from a tumor. Her world was turned upside down, and she was left confused and grieving the loss of her beloved brother. Fortunately, that is when her forever mom, Lacey, entered her story.

Lacey started following Susie's Senior Dogs (SSD) on social media many years before while she was living in New York. After being inspired by reading SSD's many posts, she promised herself that she would one day adopt a senior dog when her lifestyle was equipped to do so.

When the timing was finally right, after she relocated to South Carolina, Lacey made an appointment with the sanctuary. She had thoroughly reviewed their website and brought with her a list of the senior dogs she was especially interested in adopting. During the appointment, Jennifer, the director of the sanctuary, began considering which of the dogs would best match Lacey's personality and lifestyle.

Suddenly, another sanctuary representative mentioned Priscilla. Jennifer quickly agreed and jumped to her feet with excitement. Because Priscilla was not listed on their website, Lacey had not yet heard of her; however, she was intrigued after witnessing Jennifer's enthusiasm.

The sanctuary representatives led Lacey to meet this mysterious dog. When they arrived at her enclosure, Priscilla eagerly dashed out with her tail wagging. While her grief was still raw, it did not stop her from greeting each of them with affection. Lacey sat on the floor and showered Priscilla with attention while the sanctuary representatives filled her in on Priscilla and Elvis' backstory. It was difficult to emotionally digest; yet, hearing the story made Lacey realize that Priscilla was a dog who could really benefit from a home.

With every second that passed during their initial greeting, Lacey fell more and more in love with her. She was ready to provide Priscilla with her first real home and surround her with adoration for her remaining years. Lacey believed that it was fate that their stories intertwined when Priscilla was at her most vulnerable state, and she was thrilled to take Priscilla home with her the very next day.

Despite it being her first real home, Priscilla became comfortable in her new surroundings almost immediately. At first, she was not a huge fan of being around other dogs, but after a month of patience from Lacey, she mellowed out and now does great when interacting with other dogs.

She loves to bask on her new patio, and like most senior dogs, she can always make time for a peaceful nap. Although her arthritis flare-ups keep her from overly strenuous exercise, she thoroughly enjoys joining Lacey on relaxing walks. When she is feeling up to it, she even likes to play fetch or partake in the occasional squirrel chase.

Priscilla also likes to accompany Lacey on road trips to new places. One of her favorite destinations is the beach; she very much enjoys soaking in the salty air while walking with her paws in the sand. A naturally kind and social soul, Priscilla has a fondness for every human she comes into contact with. She lets out a whimper every time she passes someone on a walk because she is determined to meet every single human she possibly can.

Priscilla's path to finding her forever home was certainly a long journey that was laced with heartbreak after Elvis' passing, but ultimately, Priscilla has once again found peace and happiness in her new chapter with Lacey.

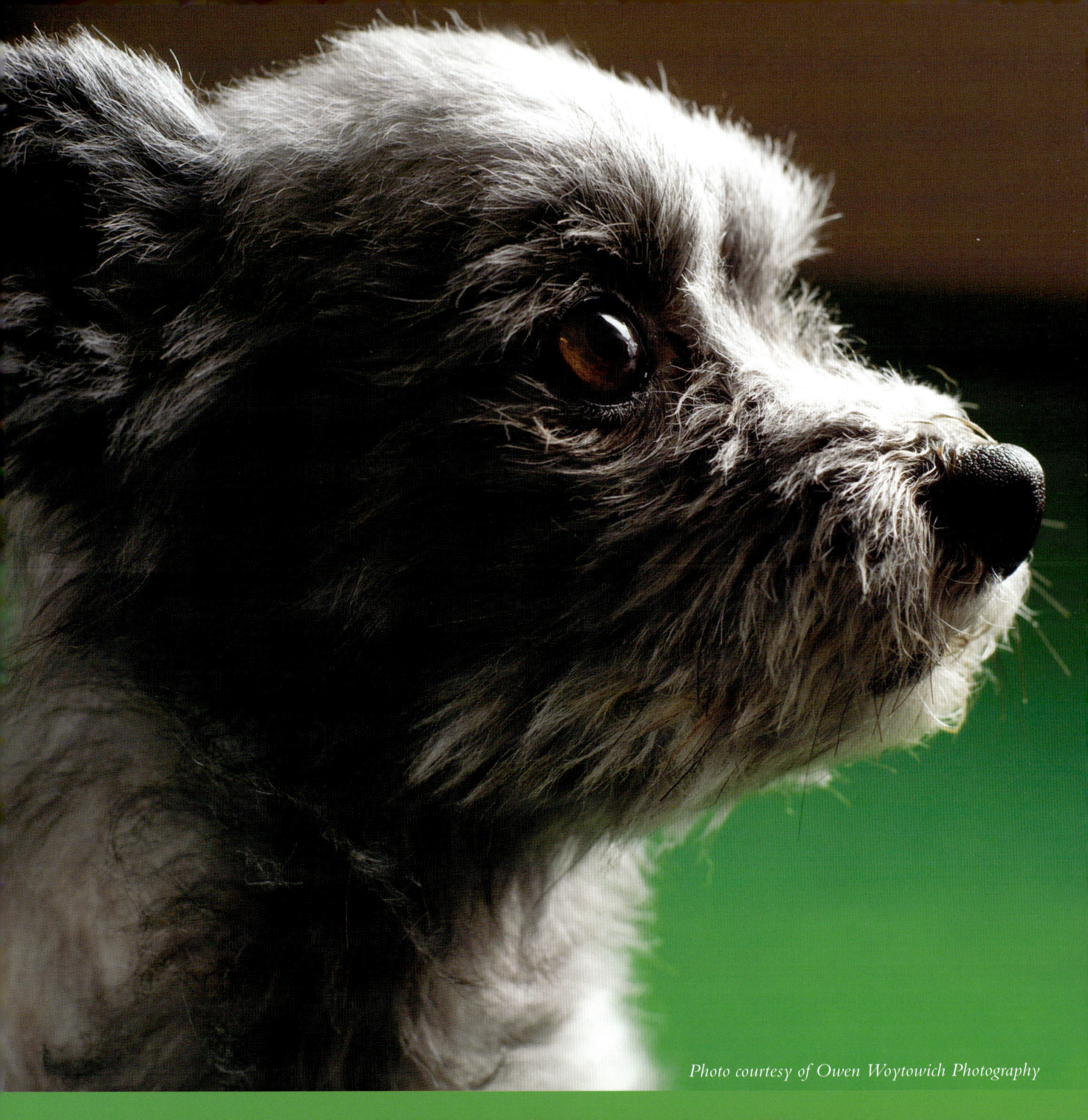

Photo courtesy of Owen Woytowich Photography

LEO, 12

At around nine years old, Leo was surrendered at a veterinary office in rural Canada and soon transferred to the Calgary Humane Society. His life prior to his surrender is a bit of a mystery, but some of his physical signs suggested he may not have been treated well; specifically, when the Calgary Humane Society took him in, he had a tumor, was unneutered, and had a severely matted, overgrown mane. After undergoing surgery to treat some of his physical symptoms, Leo recovered at the shelter and awaited his forever home.

Although married couple Koula and Neil of Alberta, Canada had been considering adding a four-legged companion to their family, their stop at the Calgary Humane Society was largely unplanned. As they walked through the shelter, they quickly spotted little Leo. He was extremely timid and cowered as they interacted with him, but despite his nervousness, he tugged at their heartstrings in a way that words cannot fully describe. They quickly decided to officially adopt him.

Koula and Neil did not plan to rescue a dog that day, let alone a senior dog, but as they reflect on the decision, they admit it certainly makes sense that they felt such a connection with an older soul like Leo. They had always inherently gravitated towards the elderly personalities in their lives, likely because the couple appreciates the calm nature, wisdom, and genuine gratitude that comes with life experience.

When Leo first arrived home with Koula and Neil, he was still very skittish. He was fearful of almost everything, including other dogs, and he would not allow anyone to pet his face. In place of a bark, he would often let out the faintest squeak possible.

Somewhere along the way, Leo became comfortable in his new chapter and, in doing so, found his confidence and voice. Now, he warms up to new friends—whether dogs or people—effortlessly. A stark contrast to his previous faint squeaks, he lets out full barks every time he hears a doorbell or a similar sound coming from the television.

Koula and Neil have discovered that, under his initial coating of fear, he is an inherently goofy, outgoing dog. Every day, Leo finds a new way to make them laugh. Some of his most memorable quirky behaviors are running around the house at full speed after going to the bathroom, and also growling at his water bowl if it's empty. He also has impeccable hearing for an old dog and will bolt to the fridge if he hears the aerosol can of whipped cream or the opening of a food package. He gets especially excited if the food packaging contains anything chicken-flavored.

A far cry from the scared dog he once was, Leo now thrives on experiencing new adventures and challenges. In their early days together, Koula and Neil took him on a weekend getaway to the Rocky Mountains, where they stayed at a high-end hotel. Although they were initially apprehensive about how he would react to such a new setting, it turns out that the "suite" life fits Leo quite well. Like true royalty, he savored many Puppuccinos and pranced around the hotel as if he had lived there his entire life. It was a sight to behold for many other hotel guests, who were stunned by the overwhelming confidence this miniature dog was projecting.

During that trip, Leo also went on many short hikes where he witnessed all types of wildlife and sniffed many new smells. After seeing how comfortable and happy Leo was during the Rocky Mountains trip, Koula and Neil have since incorporated hotel stays and visits to restaurant patios as a normal part of Leo's life.

All the new adventures aside, Leo is most content with just being near his new parents. He looks up at them every single day with a look that conveys that they are the true loves of his life. Although they can still see the former pain Leo suffered in his eyes, they are confident he is now exactly where he belongs. Koula and Neil are elated they ended up making that unplanned stop at the Calgary Humane Society so that Leo could finally enjoy the peaceful life he had been missing. They are also appreciative for all the unparalleled tranquillity, love, and appreciation he has brought into their lives.

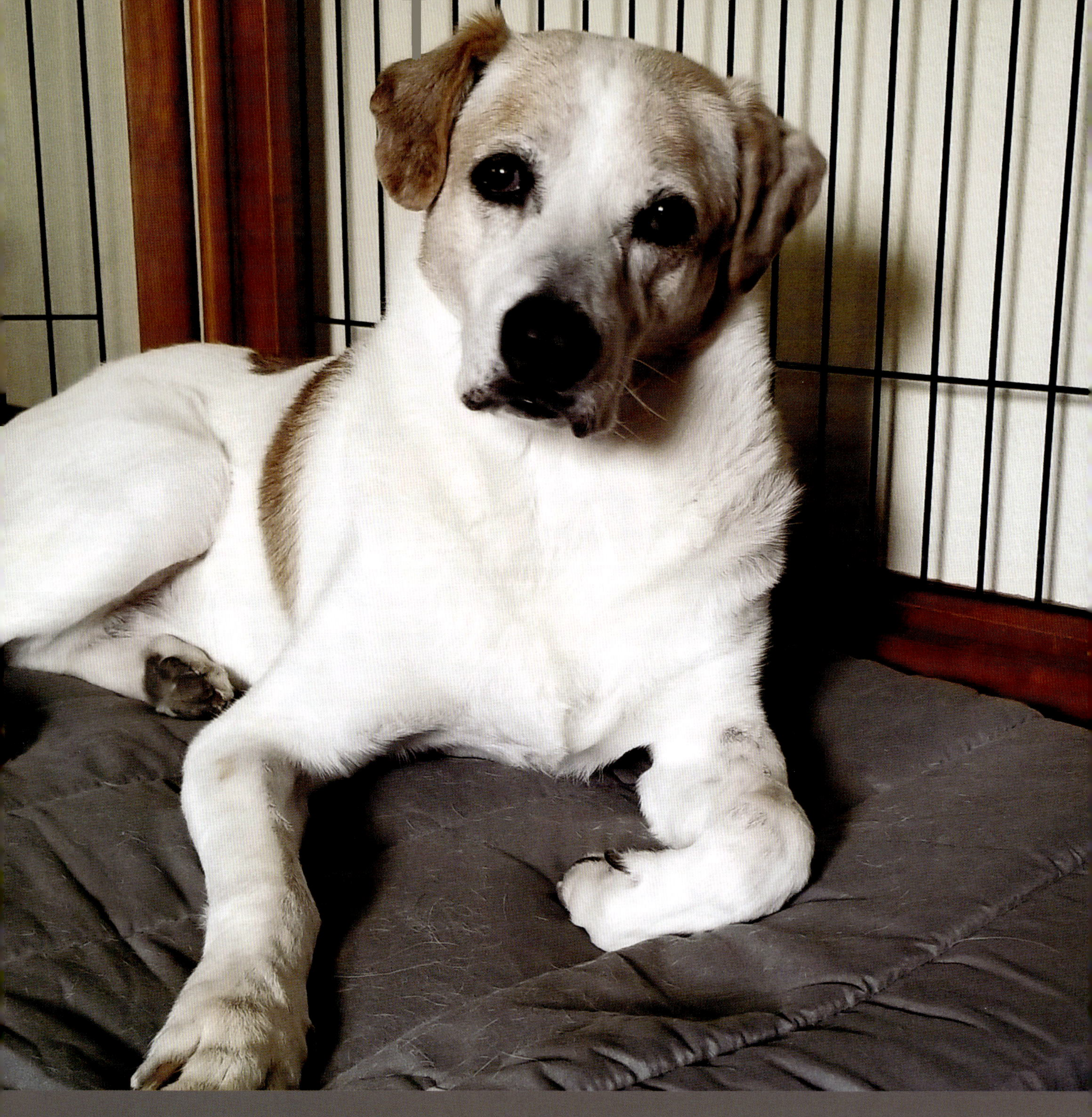

TITO, 8

Tito's adoption tale began when he was picked up as a street dog in Puerto Rico. It was not entirely known how long he had been living on the streets or whether he ever had a real home, but his rescuers were certain a better life was awaiting him. After being scooped up, he was kept in Puerto Rico for a stretch of time before being transported up to New York City.

The Big Apple was a huge contrast to his life on the streets in the Caribbean, but he seemed to transition just fine in his new foster home. After a few months in foster care, Tito's story began to circulate throughout the Instagram world.

Michelle of Ohio just so happened to follow an Instagram account for another Puerto Rican rescue dog named Millie. One day, Millie's account, run by her mom Jennifer, shared information about Tito in the hopes of helping him land a forever home. As fate would have it, Michelle saw the post about Tito as she scrolled through her news feed. The post stated he was the perfect dog whose age was likely the only reason he had not yet been adopted.

His age was certainly not a deal breaker for Michelle. Her interest continued to grow as she read about how sweet, playful, loving, and gentle he was. Two added bonuses were that, like most senior rescue dogs, he was also great on a leash and fully potty trained. Almost completely sold on Tito already, Michelle viewed some videos of him happily playing in a dog park. She fell in love with his gentle excitement, and she considered him to be the perfect combination of calm and playful.

Over the next week, Michelle continue to re-watch the videos and gaze at his photos. Because this would be her first dog as an adult, she wanted to be fully certain she and her husband, Scott, were ready to adopt him. After they agreed that a senior dog like Tito would in fact make an ideal first dog, Michelle reached out to Paws4Survival, the rescue responsible for his care. The rescue disclosed that Tito was also suffering from arthritis; however, this new discovery did not falter the couple's determination to adopt him.

They arranged a road trip from their Ohio home to New York City with every intention of bringing Tito home with them. When they finally met him in person, the connection was as instant as they had hoped it would be. Everything they had read about Tito was undeniably true, especially his sweet personality, so they quickly finalized his adoption.

Michelle and Scott spent their first night with Tito in an NYC hotel room. They got to know Tito, and he stuck to them like glue all night. The next day they embarked on their journey home, and although the trip would have typically been a nine-hour car ride, it ended up taking them nearly thirteen hours due to the many stretch breaks they took to ensure Tito was as comfortable as possible. The lengthy trip served as a great bonding opportunity; Michelle sat in the backseat for most of the trip as he gently rested his head in her lap.

When they finally arrived home, Tito quickly realized he had reached his permanent home. From that day onward, he has made himself comfortable in his new surroundings.

With each passing week, more of his personality—specifically his playful side—has surfaced.

For reasons unknown to Michelle and Scott, Tito's tail is not able to wag normally, so he makes his excitement known by slight wiggles back and forth as opposed to a full arching wag you might expect with a tail as big as his. When it is mealtime, especially if the meal includes chicken, he will also hop back and forth enthusiastically.

Overall, Tito's arthritis does not seem to slow him down too much. Some days he walks so fast that his parents have to jog to keep up, while other days he prefers to saunter and soak in all the outdoor smells.

An extremely friendly dog, Tito likes to meet everyone he comes across, with the comical exception of the delivery man and plumber. When he really wants attention from someone, he will calmly approach them and stare up with his big, lovable eyes. If his eyes succeed in earning him some coddling, he will often press his head adorably into whomever is petting him. Michelle considers this to be his version of a hug.

Because of Tito's infectiously warming presence, Michelle and Scott hope to one day spread his joy with others by helping him become a therapy dog. It is their hope that by doing this, Tito can share an important message to the universe: always accept and embrace each other's flaws and differences.

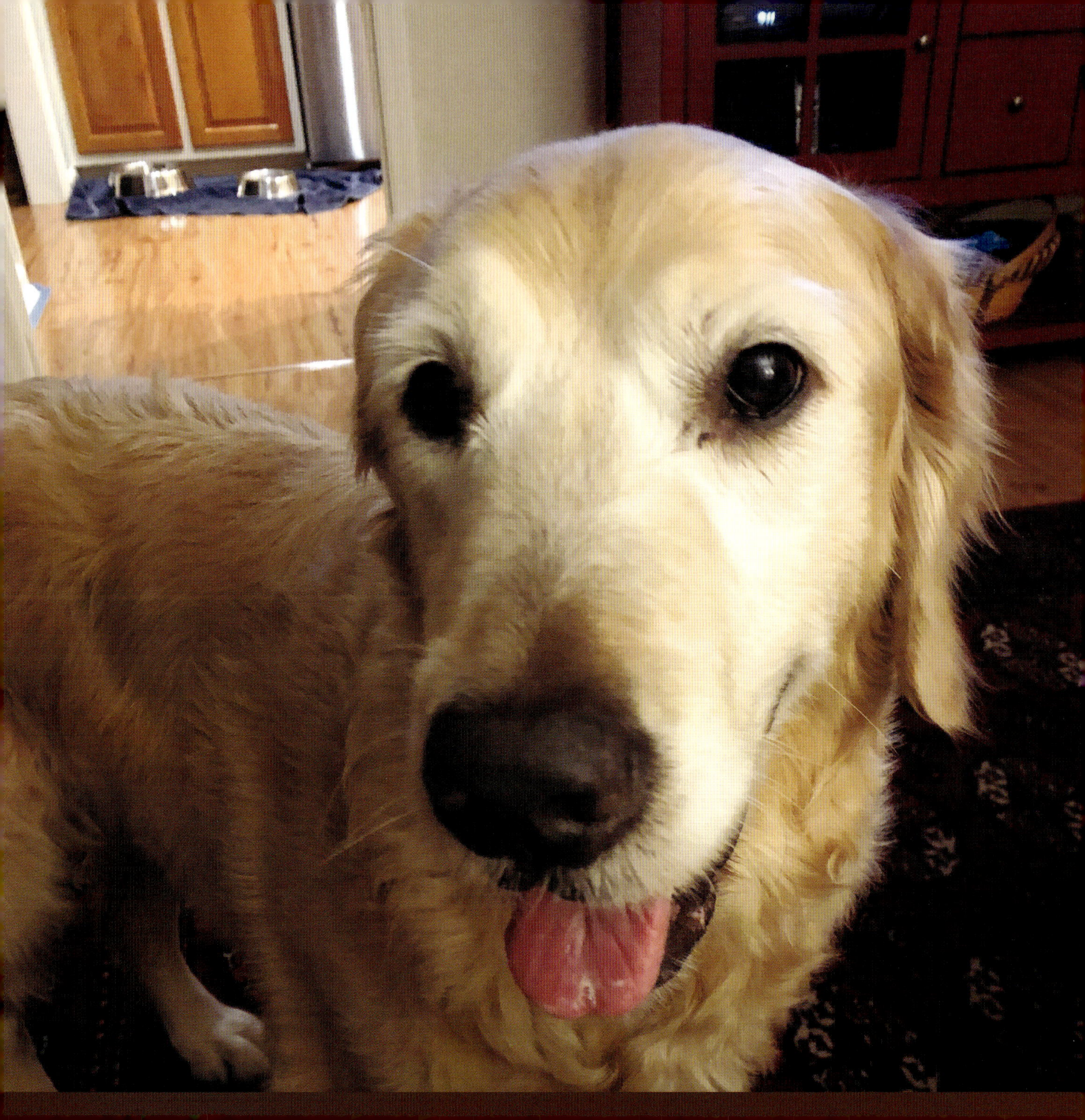

AMBER, 8

Amber lived with her original owners, an elderly couple, for many years. Over time, the couple's health declined, and their conditions began to progress quickly. Their son determined the time had come for them to move to a care facility, and sadly, Amber was not permitted to go with them. For several weeks after their transfer, Amber lived by herself in their home while someone stopped in to check on her and feed her. During this time, the family searched for a suitable new home for her.

Susan of Georgia has always considered herself a cat person. There were times over the years when she thought about owning a dog, but the timing was never quite right, especially with the personalities of the cats she owned. When her two beloved feline companions passed away within two weeks of one other, she was left deeply saddened. As she searched for a silver lining, she found herself starting to crave the companionship of a pet again. With the encouragement of many dog-loving friends and family, especially her son Clayton and niece Laura, she decided the timing was finally right for her to own a dog.

While she was not certain of the exact dog she was looking for, Susan knew two things: first, she wanted to help a dog in need and, therefore, was looking for a rescue dog; and second, she desired a dog that was a bit older because she was not quite up for all the training and supervision that a puppy typically requires.

Out of the blue, through a mutual friend, Susan connected with the son of Amber's elderly owners. Although an eight-year-old dog was not exactly what she originally had in mind, she quickly determined she had found the perfect dog. It was love at first sight. Amber was gentle and tranquil, which fit well with Susan's retiree lifestyle. In addition, her temperament and behavior made her a perfect candidate for Susan's transition into first-time dog ownership.

When Amber first came to her new home, she was extremely timid and was showing many signs of separation anxiety. Even though she was not yet overly attached to Susan in the beginning, she would still cry and crawl under the bed whenever Susan had to leave the house. It was as if she was scared of being left alone again. Now, they do a happy dance together when Susan returns home, because they are beaming with joy to see each other again!

Amber was also fearful of entering certain rooms of the house, such as the kitchen and bathrooms. After a couple weeks of coaxing and bringing her into the kitchen on a leash, she finally became comfortable. She has since become quite the sous chef in the kitchen!

With Susan's nurturing, Amber started coming out of her shell a little more each day. As she has become confident in the longevity of her new living arrangements, her trepidation has subsided, and she has formed a genuine trust in Susan. She has become protective and will bark at anyone who comes to their door. Comically, she ends up being much more receptive to male visitors as opposed to females.

Amber is very appreciative of her new fenced-in backyard, although she still prefers to have her mom accompany her each time she goes outside. This does not bother Susan one bit, and she even redecorated her patio so that she can spend more time outside. Amber also loves chasing chipmunks and birds in her yard and frequently dances on her hind legs in an effort to fly with the birds.

One of Amber's funniest quirks is that she really enjoys watching television as if she was a person. She will plop down directly in front of the screen and stare up at it with a look of genuine wonder. Amber is a *Game of Thrones* fan, but she also keeps up with the news!

Throughout her new chapter with Susan, Amber has slowly started relearning how to be a dog again. Toys are still a bit of a mystery to her, and she just stares at them while questioning what their purpose is. Fortunately, she has a doggy best friend named Boksie, also a golden rescue, who is more than happy to show her how to play with toys. She is gradually starting to pick up on her behaviors from their regular playdates.

As Amber has continued to learn and experience new things, Susan has as well. Although dog ownership is a new feat for her, she has learned so much about the benefits and companionship a dog can provide. As they look towards the future, the pair plan to keep growing together as they live out their retirements in harmony.

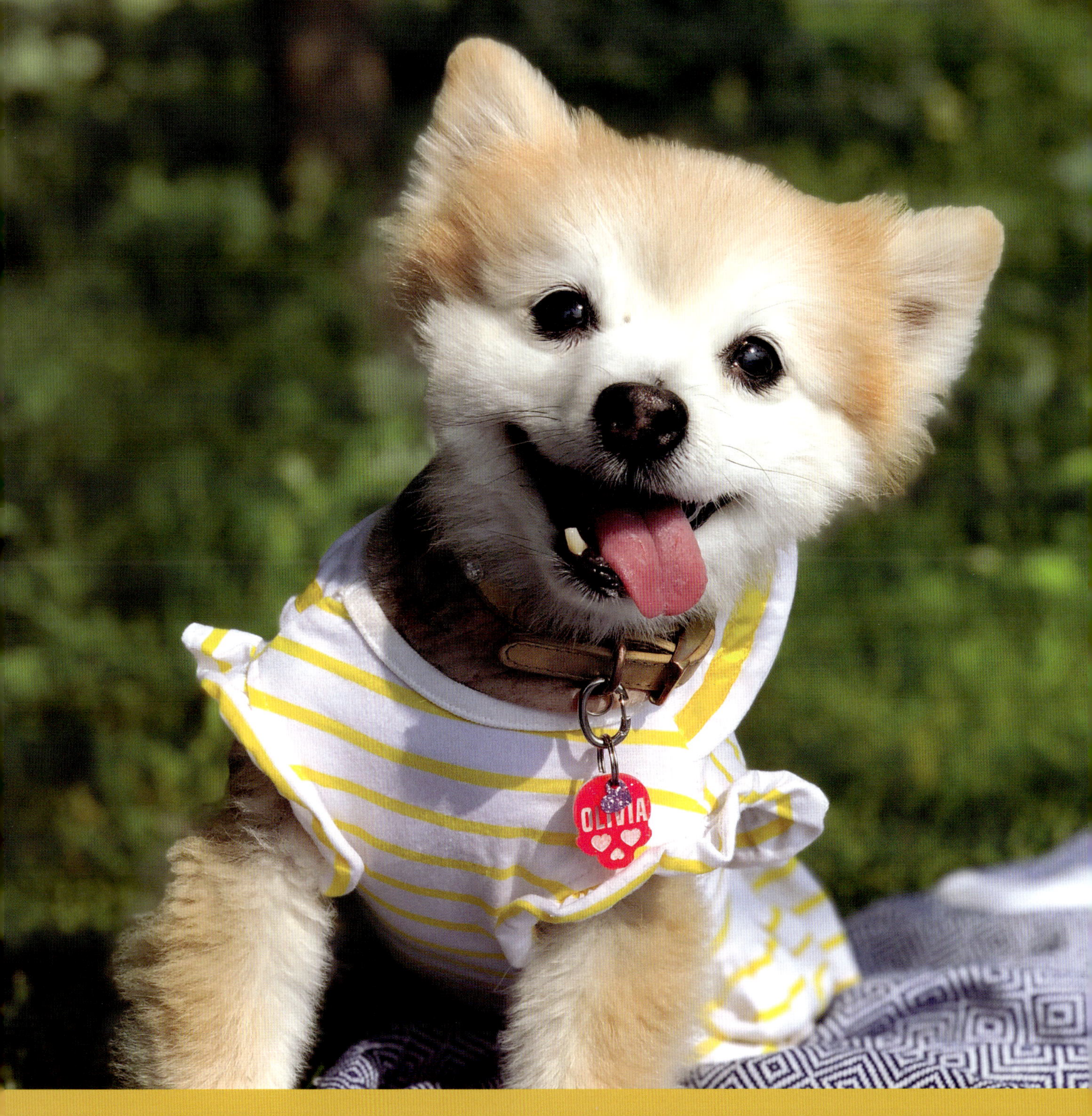
OLIVIA

OLIVIA, 13

When she was eleven years old, Olivia was tied to a pole and abandoned. While her thoughts as she waited by that pole will never be known with exact certainty, it is safe to assume she was left feeling confused and alone. Thankfully, she was discovered and picked up by animal control before being transported to an animal rescue organization called PupStarz.

After recognizing that Olivia had clearly suffered some neglect, PupStarz facilitated a veterinary check-up. The results indicated she had bladder stones and needed dental care. Olivia soon underwent surgery to remove the stone, which ended up being the size of a golf ball. She also received dental work, during which the veterinarian was only able to save one tooth. Luckily, Olivia appeared to be healthy after the operations and was ready for adoption.

Kristina of New York had just lost her dog, Oreo, to lymphoma. The pain evoked from enduring his passing was still raw, so she was not completely convinced she was equipped to adopt another dog just yet. When she came across a post about Olivia on Susie's Senior Dogs (SSD), she felt as though she already knew Olivia. Since Kristina had cared for Oreo until the tender age of fifteen, she understood the care that a delicate senior like Olivia deserved. Although she was not certain how much time they would get to spend together, she was determined to make sure that Olivia would live out her remaining golden years to the fullest.

Kristina soon contacted SSD and attended an upcoming senior pet adoption event at which Olivia would be attending. Meeting face to face sealed the deal, as their connection was genuine and definite. Kristina filled out an application and officially welcomed Olivia into her home and life that day.

It took Olivia a few weeks to acclimate to her new setting. At the beginning, she would flinch and run away fearfully any time Kristina would attempt to pet her. To help eliminate some of Olivia's initial fears, Kristina and her family presented her with lots of love and many positive words. They wanted to assure her that she was now in a safe environment and that no one would hurt her ever again.

Fortunately, their encouraging approach worked wonders for Olivia, and she soon grew into the confident and happy dog she was born to be. She is now referred to as the "shining star" of her family, and she has become an expert at seeking out attention. Sometimes, she will roll on her back and start dancing on the ground, which is a sight that is always sure to draw a crowd. Her star-like qualities are so clear that she was even selected to be a model for a canine fashion line called Rebel Dawg Shop.

A serious foodie, Olivia loves treats, especially ones that are chicken-flavored. In fact, she relishes food so much that she often herds her grandmother into the kitchen to start cooking. Kristina even has to keep an extra careful eye on her at family barbecue parties, since she is so skilled at coaxing food from people.

Olivia is lucky enough to get to accompany Kristina to work sometimes. While there, co-workers shower her with love, and in return, she runs the office like she is the boss. Of course, her favorite part of the workday occurs at lunch time.

An adventure-seeker, Olivia enjoys travelling just about anywhere, near or far. Her family jokes she suffers from chronic FOMO (fear of missing out), so much so that she jumps into any open bag she sees so that she is never forgotten. Fortunately, she is often invited to come along, and she has relished the opportunity to see many new places in her new chapter. A true travel enthusiast, she has vacationed in such places as Montreal, the Hamptons, Montauk, Charleston, Savannah, Philadelphia, and Washington, D.C. She has even had the chance to fly on a plane to some of these destinations!

All in all, Olivia's will to live is so apparent and inspiring. In spite of her unsavory backstory and heart-breaking abandonment, she maintains a beautiful spirit and positive outlook on life in her new chapter.

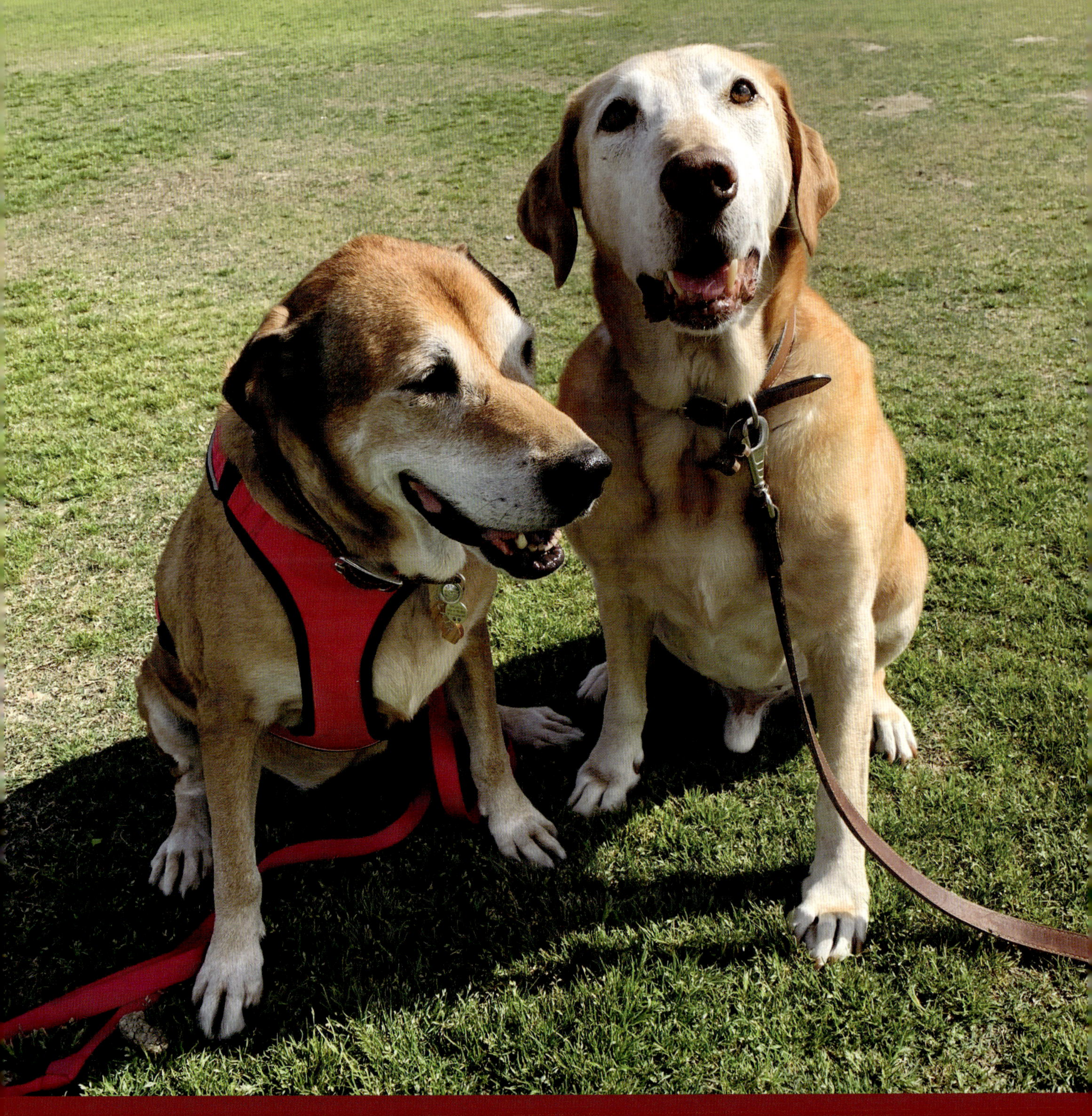

AMOS, 11; AND BLAIR, 13

When Amos the yellow Labrador Retriever was nine years old, he was surrendered by his former family at a kill shelter in Tecate, Mexico. At the time, he was in unfortunate physical shape; he was suffering from a tick-borne disease called Ehrlichia and a severe eye infection. After taking Amos in, the rescue sought help from a local animal advocate named Laura.

Laura had rescued many local dogs in the past, so it was not surprising she stepped up to help. Amos stayed with her for nearly six months while she carefully arranged treatment for his physical ailments. Once he was healthy again, she facilitated his transfer to Labs and More in San Diego with the hopes of securing him a better chance of adoption. While in the care of Labs and More, Amos stayed in three different foster homes as he waited for the right person to come along.

Molly of California had recently moved from Wisconsin to San Francisco. Shortly before relocating, she was left devastated when her chocolate lab named Bob passed away from a brain tumor. After she had settled into her new city, Molly contemplated adopting another companion and began casually browsing through dog rescue websites. She soon stumbled upon Amos' adoption profile and suddenly felt admiration for him.

Because of Bob's early passing at nine years old, Molly never got to see him through his senior years, so the opportunity to adopt another dog of the same age seemed like fate. She decided to follow her instincts and soon officially adopted Amos.

At first, Amos was extremely guarded and standoffish, likely because he was initially puzzled by his new arrangement after having moved around so much in recent months. Molly quickly discovered boundaries are important to him, so she respected his space and gave him time to settle in. Over time, his personality evolved and many of his initial mental walls have fallen.

Now, Amos is a cuddly and quirky fella who likes to play with tennis balls and stuffed toys. He loves to greet the neighbors each day. Because San Diego is largely a dog-friendly city, Molly takes Amos with her everywhere, including restaurants, hikes, errands, and many other destinations. His favorite place to go is the beach, especially after he learned to swim on a road trip to Lake Tahoe. He loves to splash in the surf and eagerly swim to retrieve tennis balls. He also has quite a knack for wearing bow ties and owns a pretty wide-ranging collection of patterns.

A little over two years after Molly brought Amos home, she decided to foster a thirteen-year-old Labrador Retriever/Rhodesian Ridgeback mix named Blair from the Frosted Faces Foundation. Not much was known about Blair's backstory, except that she was dropped off by families more than once in Los Angeles.

Blair was immediately a great fit for their little family. It turns out that, in addition to their comparable physical appearances, she and Amos have many similar interests, especially their fondness for the beach. She also likes to chase tennis balls, although she does not like to swim after them. After about two weeks as a foster, Molly decided to officially adopt Blair because she could not stomach the thought of letting her go. The trio now experience countless adventures together.

After being inspired by her wonderful experiences with Amos and Blair, Molly has become a vocal champion for senior dog adoption. She recently worked with a fellow rescue mom of a dog named Buffy, and together the two facilitated a virtual doggy wedding between Amos and Buffy.

Other dogs throughout the Instagram canine community, and even a few featured in this book, came together to serve as members of the wedding party, including Blair who was the maid of honor. Overall, the wedding was a smashing success. It not only pulled together more than $10,000 in support of animal rescue organizations, but it also raised awareness for the benefits of senior dog adoption.

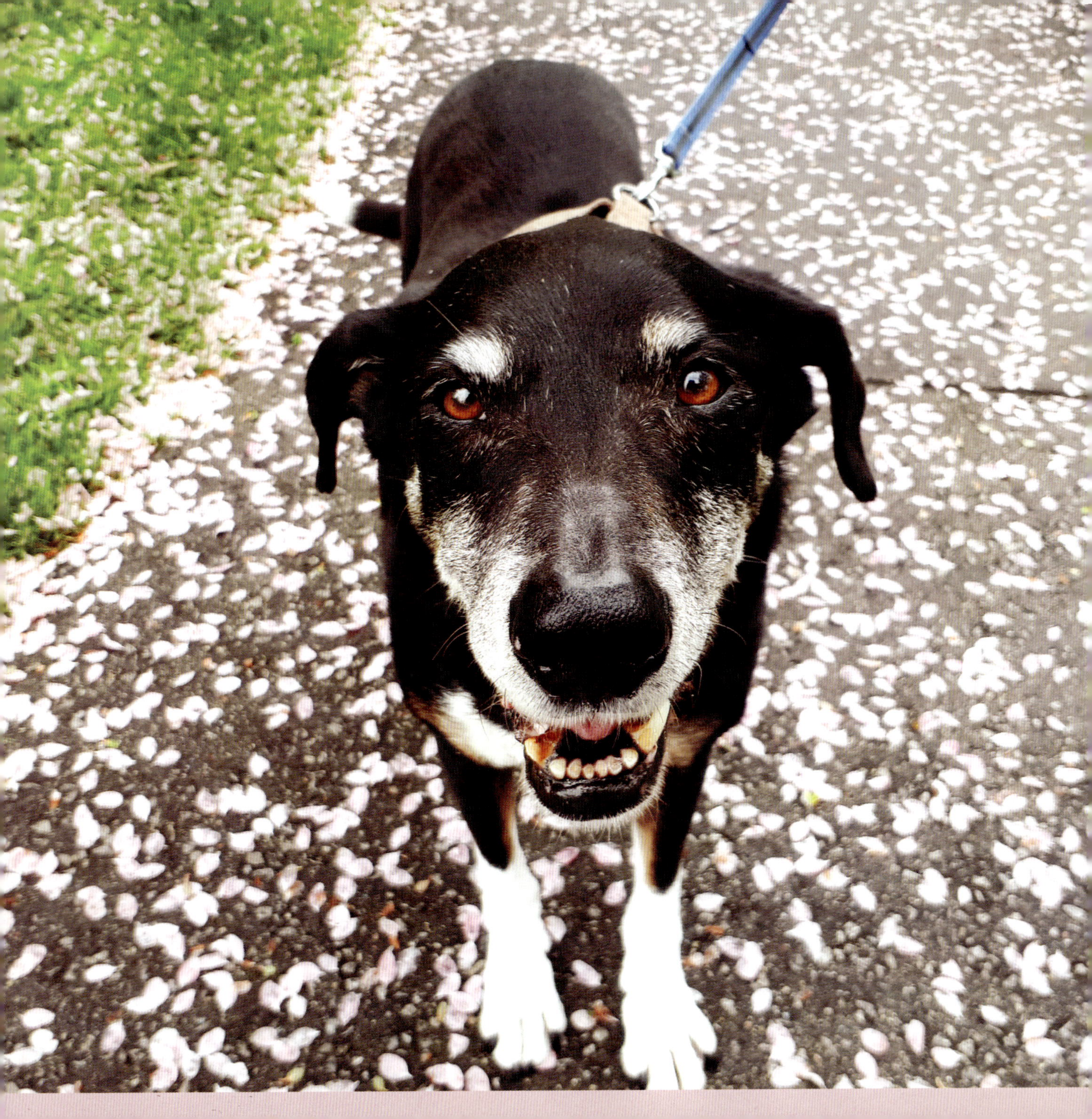

OTIS, 13

Following being found as a stray in Miami, Florida, Otis was held at a city shelter. Because he was an elderly dog and no one had come forward to claim or adopt him, he was soon placed on an urgent adoption list, which meant euthanasia was a looming possibility.

A brush of good fortune was bestowed upon Otis when he was picked up by Dog Tales Rescue and Sanctuary, a Canadian-based canine rescue organization. The rescue also picked up several other dogs from that shelter and transported them to Canada to find their forever homes.

Ray and Janice of London, Ontario had recently endured the passing of their beloved rescue dog, Parker. They had adopted Parker at six years old and were privileged to spend eight wonderful years with him in their lives.

After a few sad months of living in a home without a four-legged companion, they knew the time had come for them to open their home to another rescue dog. From their experiences with Parker, they knew peaceful old dogs are always full of love, and therefore were always worthy of adopting. In an inexplicable way, they felt Parker's memory was trying to steer them towards adopting an older dog, and they were more than willing to listen to his implicit guidance.

The couple spent a few months visiting different shelters before they eventually came across Dog Tales Rescue. At the time, Dog Tales had approximately eighty dogs who were eligible for adoption. Ray and Janice promptly reviewed all available dogs before narrowing down their list to about fifteen dogs they were especially interested in meeting.

During their adoption appointment at Dog Tales, the owner of the rescue introduced them to then eleven-year-old Otis, who was admittedly not on their initial list. When Otis walked out to meet them, he physically leaned on them to showcase his instant love for them. At that point, it was obvious to Ray and Janice that they were not there to pick a dog, but rather for a dog to pick them.

After recognizing Otis had chosen them, they soon completed the adoption paperwork and arranged to pick up Otis after a few health issues were addressed by the rescue's vet. In the seven long days leading up to the official pick-up date, the couple's minds raced with questions about how Otis would react to a new home, family, and even a new country.

When the pick-up day came, they embarked on the three-hour drive to the rescue while thoughts and questions continued to circulate through their heads. They even wondered how they were going to physically get him into the car since they were still strangers in his eyes.

Once they arrived, rescue workers brought Otis out to them. Much to everyone's astonishment, he casually hopped into their car and laid down. His calm eyes expressed he was ready to finally go home. At that moment, all worries and questions left Ray and Janice's thoughts.

Since arriving at his forever home that day, Otis has adapted quite well to his new chapter, even though it is extremely different from his life on the Miami streets. His new home is located in close proximity to many stunning parks which lay along beautiful rivers. Each and every day, Ray and Janice take Otis on several nature walks. In their early days together, the couple struggled to keep up with his fast pace on walks; however, since he has become more comfortable in his new surroundings, he now likes to take moments to saunter around and soak in all the scents left behind by other dogs.

He is an outwardly social dog who loves to meet new people. Just like that initial day at Dog Tales, Otis likes to lean up against new people as a way of saying hello. Otis is also pretty playful for an older dog; He likes to wake up early every morning and head into the family room to toss and chase his many stuffed toys. It is almost as if this morning habit is his attempt to make up for lost puppy years.

What Otis appreciates the most about his new life is that it provides him with the opportunity to just be a dog again. Completely at peace now, he never has to worry about surviving the day, and his routine is simple: eat, sleep, play, love, and then repeat.

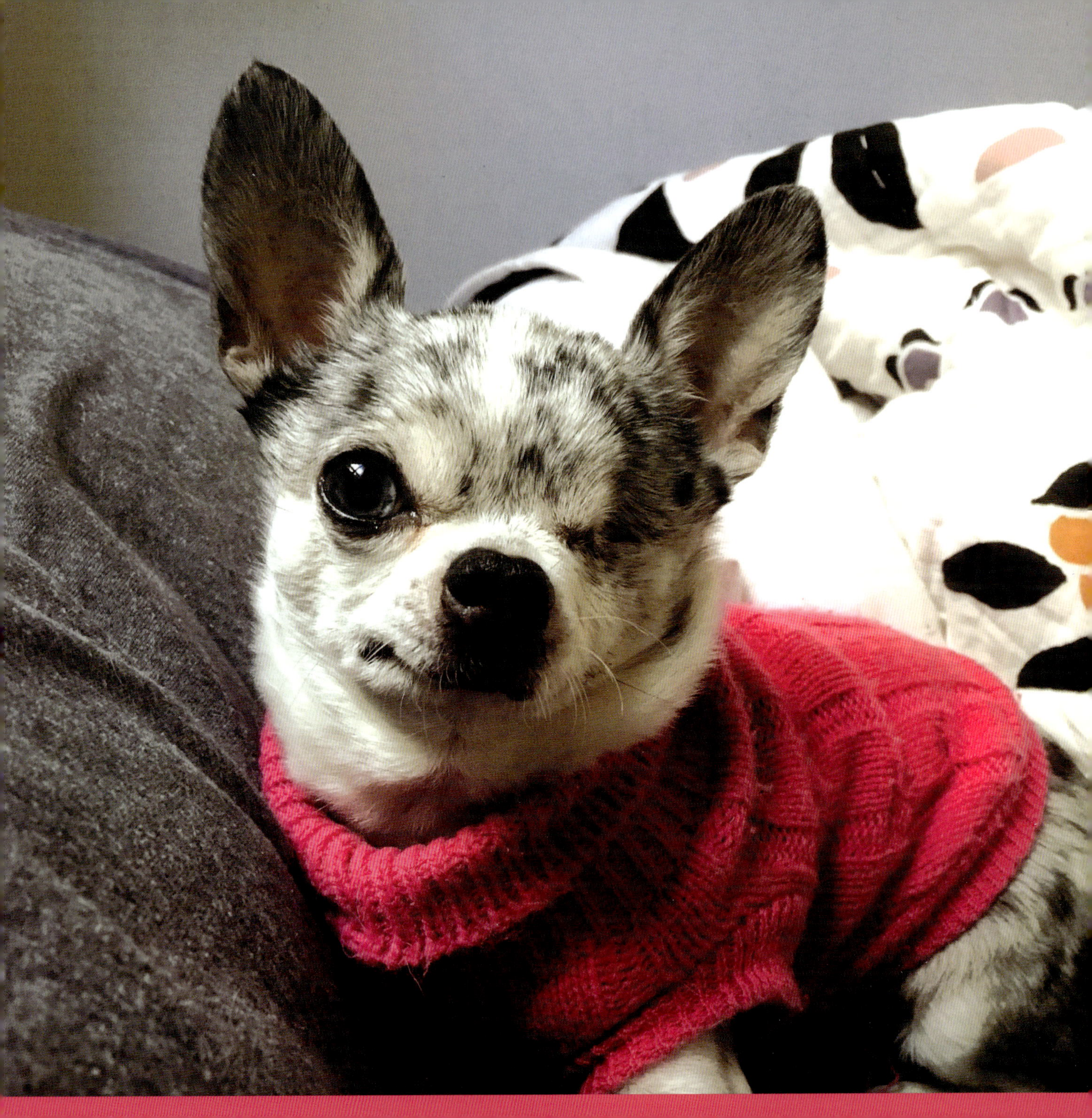

PEPPER, 9

Pepper the merle Chihuahua was found as a stray in Georgia when she was estimated to be about eight years old. At the time, she was suffering from parasites and glaucoma. Since her glaucoma had been left untreated for such a long time, it had progressed to the point where veterinarians were forced to remove her eye. After recovering from surgery, she was transported to Last Chance Ranch in Pennsylvania. Coincidentally, the rescue took in another small dog who actually had no eyes around that same time. The rescue gave them the temporary names of Wink and Blink.

Michelle of New York was already a mom to miniature rescue dog, Broccoli, and rescue cats, Frida and Ferdinand. She was considering adding another rescue dog to the mix, so she began casually perusing online rescue sites. She came across Pepper's profile and immediately experienced the "that's my dog" feeling. Pepper's age and unique look did not negatively impact her decision at all. If anything, it drew her to Pepper more.

The very next weekend, Michelle made the drive to Pennsylvania. After meeting Pepper in person, she was even more certain she had found her new companion. She filled out the adoption application, and the two headed back to New York City. Finally, Pepper's multistate journey up the East Coast had come to an end, and she had found her forever home.

During the first day in her new environment, Pepper tested every single pillow until she identified her favorite new cuddle spot. In the beginning, she was not skittish at all, but there was certainly an adjustment period with getting to know her new family, which was similar to what you might expect to experience with a new roommate. She got to know Michelle and her rescue siblings on her own terms, while they also started learning her mannerisms and personality.

At first, Pepper did experience some struggles in learning to navigate the world with one eye, but she slowly became comfortable with her new view on life. She now even uses her single eye as an advantage. For instance, to help her feel safe amid the hustle and bustle of the Big Apple, Pepper likes to have her "eye" side facing opposite to the street when taking her daily walks.

Michelle has discovered that Pepper possesses many quirky behaviors which only add to her uniqueness. She has been known to throw up on people when she gets too excited, much like a newborn baby. She likes to stand with all four of her feet on a single human hand when she is being carried. She also enjoys burrowing her tiny body into Michelle's hair when they lie down.

Because Pepper is so small, she does not fit into any doggy sweaters, which initially was a concern since the New York winters can be harsh. Fortunately, Michelle realized Pepper fits into kitten clothing quite well. Now, she humorously boasts a full wardrobe of colorful kitten clothing.

Pepper is a dog that very much likes to be close to humans. Fortunately, she is extremely approachable, and she receives a lot of attention from New York City bystanders. People of all walks of life are instantly drawn to her, even individuals who do not consider themselves to be dog people. This is likely due to the fact that Pepper knows how to turn her cute face on and work an audience. She also likes to find new humans on her own; when taking her daily strolls, she has been known to casually walk into any open door with the lights on.

After recognizing how sweet natured and social Pepper is, Michelle has started bringing her along to her job at an LGBT youth civic center. The young adults Michelle works with at the center have taken a strong liking to Pepper, and her underdog story has served as a source of inspiration to them. They love to give her treats and spend lots of time petting her, and Pepper surely relishes all the attention.

Over time, Pepper and her doggy brother, Broccoli, have formed a special bond. The two can often be found cuddling together in blankets. They also collectively hide when Michelle pulls out the vacuum or the canine nail clipper.

Although Pepper only has one eye, it is easy for her to see that her new chapter has provided her with everything she could have ever wanted, including endless love and affection from her forever family!

ACKNOWLEDGMENTS

We would like to first and foremost express our gratitude to the wonderful owners of the dogs featured in *Old Dogs, New Chapters.* Without you, there wouldn't be any "new chapters" to write about.

To our loving family and friends, we are eternally thankful for your unwavering support in all of our endeavors. We'd like to offer specific thanks to our parents, Lori, Bill, Dawne, and Steve, as well as our siblings, Emily, Caroline, Trip, Stephen, Danielle, and Dara.

Last, but certainly not least, we are extremely appreciative of the dedicated team at Mascot Books for their ongoing support in bringing our dream to life.

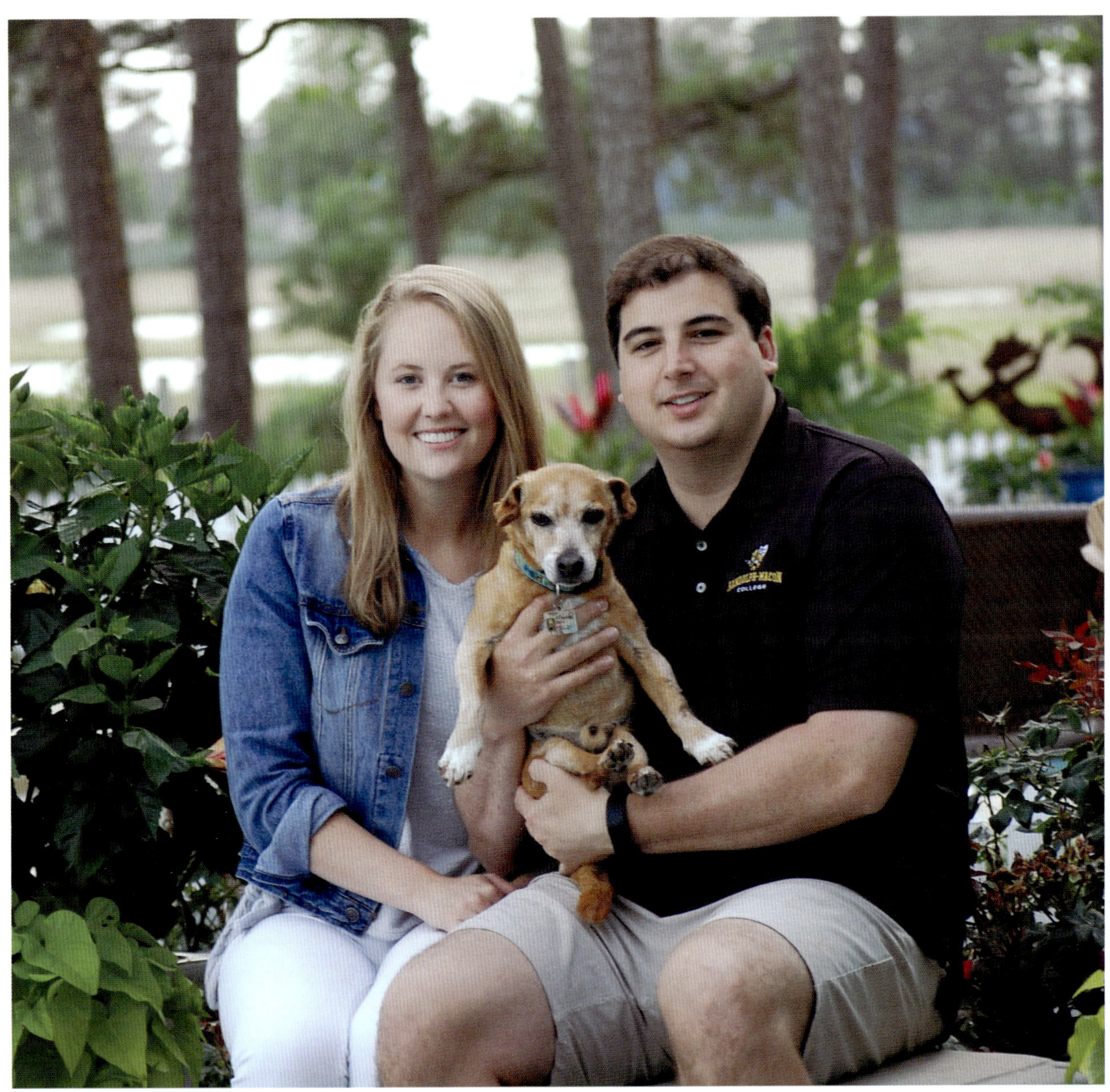

ABOUT THE AUTHORS

Alison Clary and Jason Pappas met while studying at Randolph-Macon College in Ashland, Virginia. They both grew up in large families where dogs were always present. Alison is a professional writer with a portfolio of more than one hundred published articles, and Jason manages his family's longstanding restaurant business. They live together in Ocean City, Maryland, with their senior rescue dog, Stanley.